on track ...

Eagles

every album, every song

John Van der Kiste

sonicbondpublishing.com

Sonicbond Publishing Limited
www.sonicbondpublishing.co.uk
Email: info@sonicbondpublishing.co.uk

First Published in the United Kingdom 2023
First Published in the United States 2023

British Library Cataloguing in Publication Data:
A Catalogue record for this book is available from the British Library

ISBN 978-1-78952-260-0

Typeset in ITC Garamond & ITC Avant Garde
Printed and bound in England

Graphic design and typesetting: Full Moon Media

on track ...
Eagles
every album, every song

John Van der Kiste

sonicbondpublishing.com

Acknowledgements

Thanks are due to Ian Herne, my old college friend and fellow music enthusiast of many years' standing, for regularly sharing his thoughts with me on e-mail and sending copious material and links that I would otherwise have missed; Kev Hunter, for supplying some excellent images and material from his collection; and Terry Staunton, Miles Tredinnick and Hugh McDonnell for helping with various bits, pieces and answers.

As ever, I am also indebted to my wife Kim and members of the family for unfailing support during my writing and research.

Last but not least, thanks to my ever-supportive publisher Stephen Lambe and the editorial team at Sonicbond.

on track ...

Eagles

Contents

Introduction

America was the birthplace of popular music, from jazz and swing to blues, rock 'n' roll and contemporary folk. Yet the first major names in these fields were solo acts, from Louis Armstrong, Leadbelly and Frank Sinatra to Elvis Presley, Chuck Berry and Bob Dylan. In the 1960s, it took Britain to provide the bands that would have a similar impact in terms of influence and commercial success on a global scale, from The Beatles and The Rolling Stones in the first division, with The Who and The Kinks not far behind. America's only band to come anywhere close were The Beach Boys, who would prove as durable as the best of them, although internal dissension and an excess of recreational substances, coupled with an erratic creative spark on the part of their most gifted and most troubled member, led them to rely too heavily on so-so cover versions, and held them back from fulfilling their potential. Creedence Clearwater Revival looked set to replace them before their phenomenal time at the top – and thus their career – was cut short by irreconcilable differences between their front man and the others.

It took Eagles, at the turn of the 1970s, to eclipse them and live up to their objective to become the ultimate American band. Although they went their separate ways in 1980 and took over a decade to 'get over it', in the words of one of their subsequent songs, it was a position they never relinquished. Having had a 'resumption', as they styled it, they remained together, surviving line-up changes and the death of one of their founding members. Admittedly, according to *Billboard* chart statistics, Chicago ranked second to The Beach Boys as the most successful American rock band of all time, in terms of both albums and singles. However, outside their own country, their chart achievements fluctuated, with a number one single in several territories as well as America and Britain outweighed by several modest successes and failures. Despite releasing nearly 40 albums and more than 60 singles in total over a career going back to 1969, they never matched Eagles for consistency.

Note: all Eagles records released up to and including 1980 appeared on the Asylum label. *Hell Freezes Over* was released on Geffen/Eagles Recording Co., while in Britain and Europe, compilations and reissues from around 1980 onwards were on Elektra or Warner Special Marketing. In Britain, Europe and America, *Long Road Out of Eden* was on Eagles Recording Co./Universal; *Live from the Forum* on Eagles Recording Co./Rhino/Warner, and *Live at the Forum '76* on Asylum.

The Birth of a Band

The Eagles was a name that had been adopted by several different outfits, mostly quite short-lived, during the 1950s and 1960s. A cursory glance at 45cat.com reveals that at least three American acts went by this name, the earliest being an R&B vocal group who released three singles in America in 1954. A mainly instrumental British combo made a handful of 45s between 1962 and 1964, while Belgium and Denmark could each boast their own 'The Eagles' at various stages during the decade. So could Jamaica, home to a reggae band active from around 1966 to 1976. During this period, they released eight singles in Britain, one as The Jamaican Eagles. Needless to say, none of them had any connection with the ultimate American band who styled themselves Eagles, without the definite article. None lasted nearly as long, let alone ever had a fraction of the success.

In 1971, Linda Ronstadt and her manager John Boylan needed a band for recording and touring, and engaged guitarist Glenn Frey, formerly part of the duo Longbranch/Pennywhistle, to recruit one. Frey and his former musical partner, John David Souther, had made a couple of 45s and an album on the independent Los Angeles label Amos, which during its short life also released records by country rock bands, as well as by established vocalists from an earlier era, including Bing Crosby and Frankie Laine. One of their newer bands was Shiloh, a quintet including drummer Don Henley and keyboard player Jim Norman. They issued two singles and an album on Amos, produced by Kenny Rogers, but disbanded in 1970 as they were getting no work and going nowhere, and in Henley's words, the album, 'which was awful, did nothing'.

Frey and Henley already knew each other, and from a pool of other musicians in the right place at the right time, had helped to assemble a band for Ronstadt, including multi-instrumentalist Bernie Leadon, formerly with The Flying Burrito Brothers, Randy Meisner, who had played bass guitar for Poco, and Rick Nelson and the Stone Canyon Band. They all subsequently worked with her on several live dates and played on her next album, but much as they enjoyed working with her as a person and a performer, they soon saw that their ambitions went beyond merely being someone else's backing group. Leadon credited Boylan with suggesting the idea of a separate band in the first place, telling them that if they were serious, it would be difficult to put together a better combination than they already had in place. Once they had made the decision, their split from Ronstadt was entirely amicable, they remained friends with her, and over the next few years, she would often guest with them onstage.

One of Britain's iconic singer-songwriters in the making was also in the frame, albeit tenuously. Shortly after leaving Fairport Convention in 1971, Richard Thompson was in America as a member of Ian Matthews' band, and they all met up at one stage. Richard and Ian hung out with Eagles briefly while they were still backing Ronstadt, and he was very impressed when they played him some of the songs that they had planned for their first album. Although they never asked him directly if he wanted to join them, he later heard from their management that they had considered doing so. Ian confirmed that they never gave him a second look, but they were 'very interested in Richard'. The latter would never have considered it himself, as he was intent on developing his own British style of songwriting, and joining an American country rock band, as he said, 'would not have happened' for him. Although Thompson's talents as a writer and multi-instrumentalist would have been an inestimable asset to any post-Fairport band lucky enough to secure his services, as one of the ultimate British performers in his field, it is hard to imagine him being artistically at home in an outfit which came to personify American country rock in the 1970s.

Frey was sure they could learn from the example of Poco and The Flying Burrito Brothers, both of whom had started well with everything going for them and then lost their initial momentum. They had to look good, play well, write well, have 'number one singles and albums, great music, and a lot of money'. It helped that all of them were vocalists and accomplished musicians. Frey and Henley had already written songs for their previous bands, and as contributors of original material, would undoubtedly be the joint driving force, even though several of their best-known songs would be partly penned by others. One of these writers on the periphery was Jackson Browne, a singer-songwriter and close friend of Frey. He introduced them to his manager David Geffen, who was about to start a new label, Asylum. Realising the potential, Geffen bought out Frey and Henley's existing contracts with Amos Records and signed the band in September 1971.

The following month they played their first gig. As they had not yet settled on a name, they were initially billed as Teen King and the Emergencies. A proper appellation followed, though there are several different versions of how or why they made their choice. One suggested that they called themselves after America's national bird as it would give them plenty of free publicity; another was because they liked the idea as the eagle was the bird that flew closest to the sun; another was that they were hanging out together in the Mojave Desert when they saw several soaring birds of prey overhead and Frey called out, 'Eagles!' He insisted that they should be known as Eagles, without the definite article, and the name would appear thus on all record labels, sleeves and publicity.

Eagles (1972)

Personnel:
Glenn Frey: vocals, guitars, slide guitar
Don Henley: vocals, drums
Bernie Leadon: vocals, guitars, banjo
Randy Meisner: vocal, bass guitar
Produced and engineered by Glyn Johns
Recorded at Olympic Studio, London, except 'Nightingale', at Wally Heider
Recording, Hollywood, Los Angeles, February 1972
Record label: Asylum
Release date: June 1972
Highest chart positions: Did not chart (UK); 22 (US)
Running time: 37:19

In November 1971, producer Glyn Johns, who had previously produced or engineered albums by The Rolling Stones, The Who and Led Zeppelin, was visiting America when he was asked to work with Eagles on their debut. In his memoirs, *Sound Man*, he said that Geffen was the one who contacted him for the job. However, according to an interview for Nick Hasted in *Uncut*, Johns went to a Billy Preston gig one night at the Troubadour, one of the major music venues on Santa Monica Boulevard, when Frey came up and introduced himself, said he had a band and they wanted him to produce their first album. Johns agreed to come and see them live and caught them shortly afterwards at a poorly attended club gig. He thought their sound was dreadful and the whole performance 'a mess'. The material seemed unbalanced, with Leadon, 'a great country picker', on one side of the stage, Frey, 'an average rock 'n' roll guitar player' on the other, and the rhythm section of Henley and Meisner 'being pulled in two directions in the middle'. A few indifferent cover versions, notably of Chuck Berry songs, suggested to him that they were little more than an average club band, not knowing what direction they wanted to pursue, and he returned to London, thinking he had seen the last of them.

They didn't give up. Either Geffen or Frey got in touch with Johns again, asked him to give them another chance and to come to Los Angeles so he could see them in rehearsal. Reluctantly he flew back to America and they played their set again. He found nothing to make them change his mind until they were about to leave, when one of them suggested they should let him hear one of their own compositions. Frey and Leadon grabbed a couple of acoustic guitars and they played Frey's 'Most of Us Are Sad', without bass or drums, with Meisner singing lead while the others added harmonies. The result, according to Johns, was a 'harmony blend from heaven' that sounded every bit as good as The Byrds in their heyday, and Crosby, Stills and Nash. Having four great singers with completely different voices – performing together – 'created the most wonderful sound'. They spent the rest of the day sorting through and playing him their own songs, and he realised that they were not only superb vocalists but also a much better combination of musicians and songwriters than he had appreciated at first. He found Frey and Leadon's guitars 'really refreshing', with Meisner and Henley proving a 'solid and versatile' rhythm section. They spent the next few days choosing songs for an album, and Johns then went to see them play a considerably improved set at another club.

Having agreed to produce the debut, he insisted that they should come to record in London. None of them raised any objection. On the contrary, according to Leadon, they had all wanted to record there ever since hearing Beatles and Rolling Stones records. Even so, it would not be altogether a happy experience, for in February 1972, the capital of England was a frosty, cheerless place for a young American band to come and work. Johns proved a demanding taskmaster, insisting they must work late into the night, and no drugs were to be brought into the studio. Opportunities to relax were few and far between, with all the pubs closed by the time they had completed work, food shops with a very limited choice in comparison with what they had at home, and only three television channels that all closed down before midnight. To make matters worse, the nation was in the grip of a miners' work-to-rule, with power failures at inopportune moments that might mean what had been an almost perfect performance being committed to tape would be (and sometimes was) lost in a second. Band and producer were regularly at odds over the musical approach, with Henley, in particular, resenting the idea Johns seemed to have of them as a sweet-voiced quartet of easy-listening country music balladeers.

Despite these differences, they nailed the album within about three weeks. Johns might have resented their sometimes sullen attitude, but there was mutual appreciation for the professionalism and work ethic. He had the utmost respect for their formidable vocal and instrumental talents, and the balance between all four. 'Without any one of them,' he said, 'it wouldn't have been the same.'

The band returned to Los Angeles, only to realise that the album wasn't quite finished after all. Johns was resuming work on projects with other artists in London when Geffen rang him to say they needed one more song with a lead vocal from Henley. They had tried to record 'Nightingale' during the sessions but were dissatisfied with the result, and all felt that the album was satisfactory enough without it. Someone had a late change of mind, and Geffen wanted Johns to come and try it again – on their home territory this time. Johns said no, and despite a similar call from Geffen 24 hours later, stood firm in his refusal. A few days later, Johns had a friendly but apologetic call from Leadon, who, as the one that had struck up the best rapport with their British producer had been appointed as their spokesman. He explained that Geffen had sent them back into the studio with local engineer Bill Halverson to re-record the number but were unhappy with it, and would Johns come over to America and give it another shot. He was livid with their refusal to take no for an answer and what he perceived as a lack of loyalty on their part, in going to another producer without telling him, and hung up the phone. But as he was about to go to Los Angeles anyway to master a live recording for The Who, he took the opportunity of going into Geffen's office, intending to give them all a piece of his mind. The band told him that they had been given no alternative by their label boss, who refused to release the album unless they re-recorded the song. Faced with a stalemate, Johns agreed to produce another version, which in his view, turned out no better than the first attempt, but at least satisfied everyone else.

When the album hit the record shops that June, with the lead-off single preceding it in America early the previous month, it was an instant critical success on both sides of the Atlantic. Asylum were so thrilled with Bud Scoppa's review in *Rolling Stone* that they reproduced it in its entirety in half-page press ads, while *Melody Maker*'s Ray Coleman called it 'magical, summery music that seems to have been with us for years, a lovely breath of country air and a delight from start to finish. And to think – this is their debut.' Although it never charted in Britain, it sold steadily over a long period of time and was eventually certified silver for 60,000 sales.

The album sleeve was the work of Gary Burden, a former architect turned album cover photographer and designer, based on a photo by Henry Diltz. After he had taken an image of the band sitting around a campfire, they wanted to use it as half of a four-panel poster so that the whole design would be a large square picture with an eagle flying over the desert under a clear blue sky, as seen across the outer cover. Geffen apparently thought it 'would be confusing', and without consulting either band or designer, told the printers to put the campfire shot on the inner gatefold and 'just glue it shut'.

'Take It Easy' (Jackson Browne/Frey) 3.34

The band could hardly have chosen a better song with which to launch their debut album. Inspired by a road trip through Utah and Arizona, Jackson Browne had begun writing it for his own first album. Having started the second verse with a line about Winslow, Arizona, writer's block struck and he was at a loss for further ideas. When he showed his work-in-progress to Frey, who lived nearby and had become a close friend, the latter immediately added some of his own. Browne had run out of inspiration on the second verse, which had got as far as a reference to being stuck in Winslow, where his car had broken down. Frey immediately suggested the line, 'It's a girl, my lord, in a flatbed Ford, slowin' down to take a look at me.' Browne was thrilled and wrote it down at once.

As he said in a subsequent radio interview, Frey 'finished it in spectacular fashion' and the result was a tremendous improvement on his own efforts, so he let Eagles have first option on recording it. They were delighted that such a gem had come their way. It had a momentum to it, said Leadon: 'It's cruising. We all went, "Yeah!" and started playing along.'

The passage of time often plays tricks with memories, and years later, Henley told a slightly different story. Frey was nicknamed 'The Lone Arranger' by the others as he had the perfect vision about how their voices could blend, and how to arrange vocals and music. He also had a knack for remembering and choosing good songs from other sources. Henley said that Frey remembered 'Take It Easy' as a shelved and partly written song that he had heard a while back and one day asked Browne about it.

Frey naturally took the lead vocal on the finished result, with Meisner contributing harmonies on the second verse, while Henley and Leadon restricted theirs to the chorus. The latter added lead guitar and, on Johns' recommendation, double-time banjo, which they initially thought a peculiar idea but agreed worked well when they heard the playback. As Johns said, 'It was already a great song, but that one little thing made it different.'

As an album track and also everyone's choice as the debut single (released in America in May and in Britain a month later), it immediately ticked all the right boxes, especially for a summer record, with that optimistic vibe, rich vocal harmonies and instrumentation complementing lyrics and melody to create the perfect feel-good atmosphere. Bud Scoppa's *Rolling Stone* review mentioned above called it the best-sounding rock single that year so far.

The first time through, you could tell it had everything: danceable rhythm, catchy, winding melody, intelligent, affirmative lyrics, a progressively powerful arrangement mixing electric guitar and banjo, and a crisp vocal, with vibrant four-part harmony at just the right moments for maximum dramatic effect.

Browne recorded his own version the following year on his second album, *For Everyman*, closely following the Eagles original. But theirs was the definitive, unbeatable recording.

Timothy B. Schmit, who was playing bass guitar with Poco at the time, would fondly remember hearing it at the time. When they were driving along the road to some college gig, he said, suddenly, it would be blasting out of the radio, and they would all sigh. 'This band was doing the same genre, and they were soaring past us.'

As their debut single, in America, it peaked at number 22, while in Britain, it was given generous airplay on daytime Radio 1 despite failing to chart. Over the years, it has remained one of those select non-hits that nevertheless became a staple 1970s radio oldie.

Although there's no mention of 'summer' in the lyrics, it immediately conjures up a picture of carefree life under cloudless blue skies. There is admittedly a minor allusion to pressures faced by the protagonist at the start of the song – 'I'm a-runnin' down the road trying' to loosen my load, I've got seven women on my mind' (lucky him). But after that, it's a tale of being determined to enjoy life, and 'don't let the sound of your own wheels drive

15

you crazy'. There are hints of earlier, parallel songs in different genres. In the early and mid-1960s, there were the sun-soaked, vocal harmony-enshrined anthems of The Beach Boys and their life of 'fun fun fun' on the beach, while at the dawn of the 1970s came the good-time, devil-may-care celebratory spirit of Mungo Jerry's 'In the Summertime', with its message of going out partying during the seasonal weather, when 'you can stretch right up and touch the sky'. 'Take It Easy' carried the torch further.

The song was a constant in their stage show, often as the opening number, sometimes at the end of the set or even as the encore. Frey admitted that they couldn't have ever had a better track one on the first album. 'Just those opening chords felt like an announcement, 'And now ... the Eagles."

Perhaps the last word should go to Henley. Asked by *Rolling Stone* over 40 years later for his thoughts on specific Eagles songs, he admitted that he would always remember the first time he 'heard those shimmering guitar chords in the intro pulsing through the big playback speakers at Olympic Studios in Barnes'. To him, the song had, and always maintained, a primary appeal in that it evoked a sense of motion, both musically and lyrically. 'The romance of the open road. The lure of adventure and possibility – Route 66, the Blue Ridge Parkway, Pacific Coast Highway.' Many an American writer, from Thomas Wolfe to Jack Kerouac and Wallace Stegner, had addressed the recurring theme of the restlessness of the American spirit, of a need to keep moving, especially from east to west, 'in search of freedom, identity, fortune and this elusive thing we call "home".' For him, it recalled a quotation from Thomas Wolfe's novel *You Can't Go Home Again*, published posthumously in 1940: 'Perhaps this is our strange and haunting paradox here in America – that we are fixed and certain only when we are in movement.' It illustrated the paradox of the story's hero George Webber, a writer who felt the same way, in that he always felt he was doing something with a purpose whenever he was making a train journey. Once he reached home, it was said, 'his homelessness began'.

Calling vinyl collectors: throughout the decade, Eagles singles were generally issued in Europe and Japan in picture sleeves, but not in Britain or America until 1978. The exception is what seems to be a small quantity on thin paper in Britain for promotional copies only of 'Take It Easy', and subsequently now rare. Finally, a word of warning to young guitarists on the learning curve eager to play the song: while the melody remains almost the same for the three verses and choruses, there are a few interesting variations on chords, like an extra minor, when least expected. It also breaks one of the golden rules of song by ending on a minor, not a major chord.

'Witchy Woman' (Henley/Leadon) 4.10

As if to prove that Eagles were not merely purveyors of happy country rock tunes, the second track (and the second single in America) reveals a deeper, darker tone. Henley sang lead vocal on a number he co-wrote with Leadon, a tune the latter had started while a member of his previous band, The Flying Burrito Brothers, at the start of the decade. While they were on tour, Leadon came up with the distinctive guitar riff, but never had a chance to develop it until he played it to Henley during the early Eagles days. The drummer was impressed by its haunting quality, and later called it a strange, minor-key riff that sounded like 'a Hollywood-movie version of Indian music – the kind of stuff they play when the Indians ride up on the ridge while the wagon train passes below'. They put a rough version down on cassette, and he wrote the lyrics later while recovering from flu.

His inspiration for the woman in the song was a composite. She was partly novelist F. Scott Fitzgerald's wife, Zelda, who had also been the model for several of her husband's female characters in his works. He had recently read a biography of her and was particularly drawn to the unhappy account of her drifting in and out of psychiatric hospitals as she suffered from schizophrenia or maybe bipolar disorder, whilst her alcoholic husband's health and writing career were in freefall. The other character he had in mind was the roommate of his girlfriend a year or so previously. It was a time when his generation was going through a passion for Ouija boards, séances, palm reading and all things connected with the occult, and some girls were obsessed above all with 'white witchcraft', or practitioners of folk magic for benevolent purposes, as opposed to negative witchcraft or black magic. He never took any of it seriously, regarding it as merely 'harmless fun', a phase people went through in their quest for spirituality. Henley always considered the song a personally important one for him, as it marked the beginning of his professional songwriting career. It was also the band's first Top 10 success, reaching number nine in America.

Musically it is a laid-back, brooding song that conveys an air of menace to complement the haunting vocals telling of a femme fatale who held the narrator 'spellbound in the night', who 'drove herself to madness with a silver spoon' and who has 'been sleepin' in the Devil's bed'. In a way, it anticipates and might have been an influence on the style that bands like Metallica and Nirvana would make their own.

'Chug All Night' (Frey) 3.18
Raw passion, nothing more and nothing less, is the theme of this likeable enough, if not exactly a world-beating rocker. It's an enjoyable three minutes' worth of lively, commercial rock 'n' roll meets pop, similar to the kind of material some British bands like Marmalade were specialising in at the time. An infectious harmony-laden chorus gives way to a sprightly guitar solo, which pauses briefly for a false ending before picking up again and takes the song to a tidy conclusion.

'Most of Us Are Sad' (Frey) 3.38
One moment Frey could rock out, and then suddenly, he would reveal a more vulnerable side to his writing. This ballad, with a waltz tempo, was

17

the one that grabbed Johns' attention as he was about to walk away from them, and one of the earliest original songs they worked on at rehearsals before recording the album. Leadon was particularly impressed with it, commenting that the lyric was interesting as it really expressed something truthful – 'that a lot of people probably are sad but don't express it'. Meisner was chosen to sing it as they felt his softer, higher voice brought out the mournful tone the words required. As Leadon observed, both Meisner and Henley were natural tenors, both of whom could hit the high notes without sounding strained.

'Nightingale' (Jackson Browne) 4.08
The song that had to be re-recorded, as Johns wasn't impressed with the initial take, is, to my mind, one of the stronger, more instantly commercial songs. Brisk country meets folk, it features some distinctive lead guitar and, as ever, those peerless harmonies as Henley sings, 'here comes my baby, singing like a nightingale'. After a false ending at around 3.20, it returns for some more guitar soloing until the fade.

'Train Leaves Here This Morning' (Gene Clark/Leadon) 4.13
Written about four years earlier, this country song was originally recorded on the 1968 album *The Fantastic Expedition of Dillard & Clark*. Doug Dillard was a renowned banjo player and Clark was a former member of The Byrds, while Leadon co-wrote five of the other tracks in addition to contributing banjo, guitar and backing vocals throughout. The Eagles version, on which he sang lead, follows the other closely, with the same arrangement and key, but with more emphasis on acoustic and electric guitars and vocal harmonies. As a song, it is one of those melancholy but philosophical 'time to move on after a failed love affair' lyrics, and musically has a touch of Neil Young's 'Harvest' but brisker.

'Take the Devil' (Meisner) 4.04
Rather in the vein of 'Witchy Woman', this is a slow, brooding tune with intense vocals from its writer, matching the dark mood of the lyrics – 'the wind outside is cold, restless feeling in my soul'. The first verse was accompanied by a restrained acoustic guitar and gentle patter on the drums, then stepping up a couple of gears for the more forceful rhythm section and lead guitar on the chorus. The last 90 seconds consisted entirely with a guitar break that starts softly, building up and smouldering until it fades. Some have seen the lyrics as being quasi-religious without trying to sound too stridently preachy, an encouragement to the listener to turn towards God at a time of temptation, desperation or loneliness. The lines, 'Open up your eyes, take the devil from your mind, he's been holding on to you', and allusions to a restless feeling in the soul, 'But there's no place a man can go, God, will you lead me where I roam?' hint at a search for spiritual salvation.

'Earlybird' (Leadon/Meisner) 3.03

This track is above all, a showcase for Leadon's banjo picking as well as his
second lead vocal on the album. Lyrically it seems like a light-hearted comment
on a workaholic: 'The going's getting tough, time is passing by him and he
just can't get enough'. Perhaps significantly, this is the first of their lyrics to
refer to the bird from which they took their name: 'the eagle flies alone and
he is free'. It could have been improved if the tuneless whistling effects on the
intro that resurface later in the song had been dispensed with, but by way of
compensation, Frey unleashes some fine slide guitar towards the end.

'Peaceful Easy Feeling' (Jack Tempchin) 4.20

An occasional solo performer and guitarist, Tempchin's reputation rests
largely on the songs he wrote or co-wrote for and with the band. The sweet
country near-ballad that would become the third single in America (but not
in Britain), peaking like the first at number 22, gives Frey his last lead vocal
on the album. He said that at the time, Poco was his main role model as the
band to emulate, largely as their vocals were so perfect. They had always
loved The Byrds and The Beach Boys, but Poco most of all, and he 'wanted
to go beyond them too'. The fact that both their bass players had left Poco to
join them reinforced the connection.

Tempchin wrote it after a gig at a small club in California, during his first
time in the desert, and when he looked around him, he found the view of the
stars amazing. He had a passing crush on a waitress working there, sadly not
reciprocated when she went home that night without him, so he slept on the
floor in the club with his guitar instead of her. But at least he got a song out
of the experience, about a yearning 'to sleep with you in the desert night with
a billion stars all around'. When Frey heard him play it during a session at
Jackson Browne's house, he begged to be allowed to try it with the band, and
brought him a tape of their rehearsal demo the following day. Tempchin was
astonished at how good they made it sound. Their finished version radiates
peace and contentment, with steel, lead and acoustic guitars complementing
each other as well as the vocal harmonies providing a perfect setting for
Frey's lead. The song always remained one of his favourites for its happy,
country rock quality coupled with a bittersweet irony.

Some 25 years later, the song received a new lease of life of sorts via the
movie *The Big Lebowski*, a black comedy crime drama. One of the main
characters gets into a cab, just as it's playing on the radio. 'I hate the fuckin'
Eagles, man,' he mutters and the driver, evidently a passionate fan, throws
him out. Frey apparently failed to see the funny (not to say flattering) side of
it and was unimpressed.

'Tryin'' (Meisner) 2.54

Like 'Chug All Night', this closing tune confirmed that the band may not have
been a match for Johns' most illustrious other clients, The Stones or The Who,

but they could still rock out. This makes more demands on Meisner's vocal range than the other two on which he sings lead, while a guitar solo takes it up yet another notch about midway through and it barely lets up until the final chord dies away. In Britain, it was the second single from the album, released in February 1973, but with no radio airplay, it passed more or less unnoticed.

Significantly, Meisner had three lead vocals on the album, as did Frey, with Henley and Leadon two each. Scoppa, who followed up his initial 1972 review with a retrospective piece for *Uncut* many decades later, observed that in their early, more democratic days, they had just made 'the most balanced album they'd ever release'.

Related track:
'Get You in the Mood' (Frey/Jackson Browne) 3.52
Recorded at the sessions for the first album, this failed to make the cut but appeared on the reverse of 'Take It Easy'. It is unique among the band's catalogue in being their only orphan B-side, at least until a festive non-album Christmas single in 1978. A million miles away from country rock, it's a slow, sensual track with Frey singing lead again, and soulful harmony vocals on the chorus. There's subtle use of tremolo on the guitar intro, and after a song that calls the measured, even smouldering pace of Buffalo Springfield's 'For What It's Worth' to mind, it ends on a tingling guitar solo. It would have been an obvious choice as a bonus track for CD reissues but never became one, making its first appearance on album (vinyl and CD) as part of the mammoth *Legacy* boxed set in 2018.

Desperado (1973)

Personnel:
Glenn Frey: vocals, acoustic and electric guitars, keyboards, harmonica
Don Henley: vocals, drums, acoustic guitar
Bernie Leadon: vocals, electric and acoustic guitars, banjo, mandolin, dobro
Randy Meisner: vocals, bass guitar
Jim Ed Norman: string arrangements, conductor, piano ('Saturday Night'), electric piano ('Outlaw Man')
London Symphony Orchestra: strings
Produced and engineered by Glyn Johns
Recorded at Island Studios, London
Record label: Asylum
Release date: April 1973
Highest chart positions: 39 (UK); 41 (US)
Running time: 35:40

On their second time around, Henley and Frey wanted to make an album, based around the story of a Wild West outlaw gang, the Doolin-Daltons. Johns loved the idea and noted afterwards that they had a great time making it. But it was created during a difficult time. The band had enjoyed the freedom of being part of a small artist-orientated company label, and were concerned when Geffen sold Asylum Records to Warner Bros., a highly lucrative deal from which he profited greatly while the band received nothing.

Frey and Henley had already written 'Desperado'. The lyrics could mean several things at once, although the generally accepted interpretation is that it concerns a hard-bitten but lonely cowboy who's not getting any younger, and is being urged to 'come down from [his] fences', look up to the rainbow above him and let himself find the right girl before it's too late. From this, the idea gradually grew of a thematic cycle, a concept album, in Henley's words, 'our big artistic statement on the evils of fame and success, with a cowboy metaphor'. While based around the exploits of the legendary Dalton Brothers gang, it would also make indirect references to the business merger of which they had become an unwilling part. Like many a band member before and after them, they saw themselves as young radicals, rebelling against the music business with which they had a love-hate relationship, but of which they still remained part – or as Joe Strummer would later put it, 'turning rebellion into money'. The point seemed lost on Geffen, who was seemingly unaware of their irritation with him, and loved the idea, perhaps seeing it as an American, 1970s answer to *Sergeant Pepper*. Ironically, a similar project was done not long before. It had taken a British partnership, Elton John and Bernie Taupin, to make a far more successful Wild West-themed album, *Tumbleweed Connection*, in 1970.

Although Eagles' initial working relationship with Johns had not been totally satisfactory, he was also enthusiastic about the idea and keen to

21

produce them again. The band, plus the other main members of their creative hub, Browne and Souther, plus friend and roadie Tommy Nixon, got together and wrote several songs that expanded on the theme. One song from outside, 'Outlaw Man' by fellow Asylum artist David Blue, was felt appropriate for the concept and they decided they would cover it for the album. Nevertheless, it was apparent that Frey and Henley were becoming the Lennon and McCartney of the band, collaborating and writing more and more of the songs between them. They admired the way that both of the Beatles' front men had written so many songs together in the early days, sitting in the bedroom of one or the other, trading lyrical and musical ideas with guitars in hand. At the same time, they both saw parallels between themselves and their Liverpudlian exemplars, whom Henley said many years later were 'still [my] favourite group in the entire world'. He, and maybe the other future Eagles, had been among the millions of American teenagers who had watched and would never forget the Fab Four's TV appearance on *The Ed Sullivan Show* in February 1964. Frey regarded himself as the McCartney figure to Henley's Lennon. Henley, he said, was …

… more topical while I was a little bit more easygoing. I was the one more apt to sit down and write a love song, while Don was more apt to chew somebody off. But, even though Don was portrayed as the serious guy, I know for a fact that he also had a great sense of humour.

On occasion, Henley and Frey would add to or alter songs begun by Leadon or Meisner on the old basis of 'write a word, get a third [of the royalties]', although their input was more considerable than just a word or two. Leadon wrote a couple of tracks on his own and contributed to another, while Meisner collaborated on two, but the final songwriting credits would show who were now the two driving forces. Significantly, Henley had only had one joint writing credit (and one individually) on the first album, while the other three each had three joint or solo credits. The drummer upped his game sharply after that. Another notable factor was that Henley and Frey would frequently create and then write most of the songs between themselves, but were less self-contained than the English moptops and would sometimes rely on a third party, such as Jackson Browne or J.D. Souther, to write a bridge or help with the final touches in some other way.

With new material ready to go, they returned to London and spent four weeks during the spring of 1973 at Island Studios, with Johns back in the producer's chair. Despite their lack of enthusiasm for London, all four members remained focused and enthusiastic, and Johns said they were all so pleased with the results that after he played it back to them as an entity for the first time, they carried him out of the control room on their shoulders in celebration. He was also pleased with having been able to play a suitably diplomatic role, encouraging the involvement of Leadon and Meisner, as he sensed that the other two were exerting more and more control over the creative process and suspected that cracks were beginning to appear in the relationship.

For the photo on the back sleeve, everyone got into the spirit of a gang shoot-out, with the Doolin-Daltons being captured and shot dead. Costumes were hired from a rental place that regularly supplied costumes for the big western movies, including several that starred John Wayne, and the band were so enamoured with the ones they wore for the photo shoot that they never returned them. Asylum presumably paid the bill. The victorious posse in the picture, standing at the back, included roadie Tommy Nixon, designer Gary Burden and Glyn Johns, while the victims lying at their feet were the band, plus Browne and Souther. One wonders whether they would have got away with such an image for the record in the 21st century.

The record was an artistic and critical success but performed below expectations. American sales were steady for some time and, like the first album, it eventually went platinum (two million sales), but during the first few weeks of release, it suffered through lack of promotion, largely as Geffen was more concerned with finalising the sale of Asylum to Warner Bros., and also signing Bob Dylan for two albums. (It never lasted – Dylan returned to his old label Columbia a year later, and stayed there.) Johns felt that the band partly blamed him for the comparative failure. Another reason was probably the lack of success for both singles taken from it, with 'Tequila Sunrise' and 'Outlaw Man' only reaching numbers 64 and 59, respectively. Although it narrowly missed the Top 40, some fans regard it as the semi-undiscovered classic album they never bettered throughout their career.

Henley always rated the record highly. Some years later, he told *Rolling Stone* that it was 'a commentary on consequences, on the thing that some call "karma". It's also a meditation on the repercussions of living an isolated existence that rejects the idea of community, a life devoid of love and compassion, hence the final lines of "Desperado".' Moreover, he saw an affinity with the anti-heroes they were singing about. In another interview with the same journal, he stated that the basic premise was that, like the outlaws, rock 'n' roll bands lived outside the 'laws of normality' and were not part of 'conventional society'. It was their way of life to go from town to town, collecting money and women …

… the critical difference being that we didn't rob or kill anybody for what we got; we worked for it. Like the outlaws of old, we fought with one another, and occasionally with the law. But I think the overriding premise was that fame – or notoriety – is a fleeting thing.

'Doolin-Dalton' (Frey/J.D. Souther/Henley/Jackson Browne) 3.26

The opening song was inspired by a book given to Browne about the real-life Dalton Brothers and their partner in crime, Bill Doolin, a gang of outlaws and bank robbers who lived in the 19th-century world of 'easy money, faithless women and red-eye whisky'. As they began to write the song, the theme turned towards mythical majestic images of the Great American Southwest.

Musically this sounds remarkably like Neil Young, with Frey's plaintive vocal, ragged harmonica and acoustic guitar dominating the first minute or so until the rhythm section and vocal harmonies join in. Henley's rasping vocal takes centre stage for the last couple of lines of the song. Leadon said the band had known and been friends with contemporaries who had been brought before the courts for smoking pot or avoiding the draft, so they 'felt some affinity with the concept of being outlaws'.

'Twenty-One' (Leadon) 2.11
Leadon follows his vocal, banjo and dobro leading on a song about Emmett Dalton, the baby of the Doolin-Dalton gang. He was aged 21, 'as young and fast as I can be', when they carried out a bank raid in Coffeyville, Kansas, in October 1892. Four of them were killed, while Emmett was shot several times but merely wounded and was sentenced to life in the Kansas penitentiary, serving 14 years before being pardoned. 'Someday I might settle down', runs one line of the song, and after moving to California, he did indeed – he became a real estate agent, author and actor, dying of natural causes in 1937, aged 66.

'Out of Control' (Henley/Frey/Tom Nixon) 3.04
Next, the outlaws ride into town, hell-bent on an evening of drinking, gambling and womanising – basically getting a little out of control. Alternatively, it could be the story of a gang whose best days are behind them, running amok on the path towards inevitable destruction and death. Whatever the meaning, the result is undoubtedly as raucous as the band ever got in the recording studio. This is their 'Communication Breakdown' moment, as they rain down on the unsuspecting listener a no-holds-barred distorted wall of sound, with a battering ram of nasty (in the best sense) strident guitar chords, a barely suppressed scream and a hoarse vocal from Frey that sounds like British punk rock some three years before The Damned's first 45. Could it have inspired Elton John's 'Saturday Night's Alright For Fighting', which was recorded only a few weeks after the release of *Desperado*? A false ending just after two minutes is followed by a coda of chaos in which Frey continues to holler while still determined to compete with Henley as to who gets the last guitar chord or the final crash on the cymbals.

'Tequila Sunrise' (Henley/Frey) 2.52
This could hardly be more different to the preceding track. Along with the album's title track, it was one of the first songs written by Frey and Henley as a partnership, not long after they had recorded the first album and returned from London. While they were mulling over ideas at the latter's home, Frey came up with a guitar lick that he thought was partly Roy Orbison, partly Mexican music, and suggested they should develop it as a new song. The

majority of it was Frey's work, and he took lead vocal. Acoustic guitar, peerless harmonies and a suitably restrained rhythm section, including maracas, are overlaid with a sparingly tender lead guitar that has its finest moment in a short and sweet solo.

Frey was uncertain about the title as he thought it might be rather too obvious or too much of a cliché, bearing in mind the then popularity of the cocktail from which it took its name. Henley suggested otherwise, telling him that it was just perfect: 'you've been drinking straight tequila all night and the sun is coming up'. Lyrically, it's the song of 'a hired hand', 'a lonely boy in town', drinking at the bar every night when she sun goes down while the object of his affections is out on the town, maybe sleeping around. All he needs, perhaps, is to 'take another shot of courage' and declare his feelings for her – 'wonder why the right words never come'. Henley said they used to refer to tequila as 'instant courage'. While out on the town, they desperately wanted to talk to the ladies, but so often they never had the nerve, 'so we'd drink a couple of shots and suddenly it was, "Howdy, ma'am."'

Frey thought the song was one of his best. For him, the goal of the songwriter was to make a song appear seamless. Nothing should sound forced, he said. 'Tequila Sunrise' was written fairly quickly, 'and I don't think there's a single chord out of place'.

'Desperado' (Henley/Frey) 3.36

The title track was a song that Henley had begun writing about four years earlier, about a friend of his, with the opening line, 'Leo, my God, why don't you come to your senses.' He played and sang what he had to Frey, remarking that it made him think of Ray Charles and Stephen Foster. 'It's really a Southern Gothic thing, but we can easily make it more Western.' Frey immediately set to work and completed it. As Henley later observed, it marked the beginning of their songwriting partnership, and the point at which they became a team.' I think I brought him ideas and a lot of opinions,' said Frey, 'he brought me poetry – we were a good team.'

Lyrically, it has a theme not so far removed from that of 'Tequila Sunrise'. In part, it's a sad song about the lonely life of a cowboy (one of the Dalton gang, it is assumed) on the trail, prolonging his youth and shutting his eyes to what the future might hold. Meanwhile, a kindly friend or relative urges him to give up his life on the wrong side of the law and settle down – 'come to your senses, you've been out ridin' fences for too long now'. The desperado is not getting any younger, and it's time he sought relief from the rainbow up above him. Guitars take a complete rest as a stately piano intro precedes Henley's vocals, with strings coming in on the second verse, impassioned drums on verse three, as the orchestra soar to a crescendo, a hint of call-and-respond vocal towards the end, and a gentle finish from strings and piano. It was, in a way, the band's own 'Bridge Over Troubled Water', and immediately took on such a stature of its own, with regular airplay over the years, that many people assume it was a hit but can't recall when. Its unavailability as a 45 may have helped to ensure further sales for the album.

High-profile contemporaries queued up to record the song themselves. Foremost among them was their former comrade-in-arms Linda Ronstadt, who featured it on her fourth album, *Don't Cry Now,* released later that year, and on a subsequent B-side in America. (It was an A-side in Britain a little belatedly in 1976, by which time its moment had doubtless passed.) Yet as Henley readily admitted, her regular performances of the song onstage helped to give it a higher profile. In 1975 it had been an album track on The Carpenters' *Horizon*, and two years later did the same on Henley's old producer turned major country star Kenny Rogers' *Daytime Friends.*

'Certain Kind of Fool' (Meisner/Henley/Frey) 3.02
Initially written by Meisner, who sang lead vocal, and completed by Henley and Frey, the subject of this was the boredom, longing and restlessness of young men in the last days of the western frontier. Some have seen it as open to dual interpretation, being about a youth who wants to be famous and recognised wherever he goes, then realises that fame is a double-edged sword, in other words – be careful what you wish for. As a kid, he wanted a gun so he could learn how to use it and be an outlaw; or did he want a guitar to further his dream of becoming a rock star? At any rate, he was 'a certain kind of fool who liked to hear the sound of his own name, got his poster on the storefront, the picture of a wanted man' – and, as a result, ended up on the run. A crisp acoustic rhythm guitar is at the forefront, with a brief but powerful guitar break halfway through.

'Doolin-Dalton' [instrumental] (Frey/J.D. Souther/Henley/Jackson Browne) 0.48
Three-quarters of a minute of banjo and guitar wizardry (yes, four joint writers were credited for a mere fragment), that make a good breathing space between tracks as it crossfades into the next.

'Outlaw Man' (David Blue) 3.34
The album's second single and the only song in which none of the band had a hand in writing came from fellow Asylum artist David Blue, formerly part of the Greenwich Village folk scene alongside the likes of Bob Dylan, Phil Ochs and Tom Paxton. Blue recorded eight albums during an 11-year recording career before becoming a movie actor for the rest of his short life, but this remains his greatest claim to fame. He had recorded his own version on the album *Nice Baby and the Angel*, which included Frey on backing vocal, earlier that year. They had all heard it prior to release, and Frey said he thought it would fit in well with the concept of their own second album. As it was quite an up-tempo tune and they 'weren't writing very many at the time', they considered it an ideal choice. Frey sings the vocal on this lively tale of an outlaw whose

legacy was the highway, who carried a Bible in one hand and a gun in the other. Again it bears more than a passing resemblance musically and vocally to Neil Young, while some sharp guitar soloing and an animated rhythm section with Meisner's bass more prominent and Henley's drumming more frantic than usual, gives the impression of speeding up about halfway through.

'Saturday Night' (Meisner/Henley/Frey/Leadon) 3.20

This bittersweet composition was largely by Meisner, with contributions from the other three. It was inspired by his musing one evening and the line 'Whatever happened to Saturday night?' just came to him. In his younger days, he would be out partying and enjoying himself. So what happened? The obvious answer came back: 'You're *older* now.' From it developed a song of love and loss, memories of romance and the gift of a ring to his sweetheart so many years ago, and now she passes the time at another man's side. The final line in the song, 'Someone show me how to tell the dancer from the dance' has puzzled some listeners, who suggest that the now middle-aged man on his own is wondering whether it was marriage (the dance) or the woman he married (the dancer) that failed him. For the backing, all it needs is acoustic guitar, bass, some exquisite mandolin from Leadon, and as ever, a touch of breathtaking vocal harmony in the chorus.

'Bitter Creek' (Leadon) 5.00

Leadon's second solo composition celebrates the short, violent life of another member of the Doolin-Dalton gang. George 'Bitter Creek' Newcomb survived several shoot-outs before his luck ran out; he was wounded, went on the run and was subsequently shot dead in a separate outlaw attack. The lyric is an optimistic one, finishing on a note of triumph as the hero predicts he will 'win the race', which he never did in real life. It is the longest song on the album, with Leadon's lead vocal backed up by harmonies from the others, and a couple of acoustic guitars, one playing the chords while the other adds some unobtrusive picking, with only the lightest of touches from the rhythm section.

'Doolin-Dalton/Desperado [reprise]' (Frey/J.D. Souther/Henley/ Jackson Browne) 4.50

Two of the tracks are rearranged for a reprise, as a grand finale for the album, with Henley on vocal. At the start, the stage is set for another showdown. Whether the desperado perishes or lives to fight another day, maybe even a new life, is for the listener to judge. His twisted fate has found him out, he sealed his fate up a long time ago, and now there's no time left to borrow – or is there? Musically, it follows the measured, mournful pace of the original 'Desperado' song earlier on, although with a busier instrumental backing that includes drums, acoustic guitars, banjo and dobro as well as strings, as it fades into the distance on harmonies for the title repeated several times.

On the Border (1974)

Personnel:
Glenn Frey: vocals, acoustic, electric and slide guitars, piano
Don Henley: vocals, drums
Bernie Leadon: vocals, electric and acoustic guitars, banjo, pedal steel guitar
Randy Meisner: vocals, bass guitar
Don Felder: lead and slide guitars – 'late arrival' ('Already Gone' and 'Good Day in Hell' only)
Produced and engineered by Bill Szymczyk, except Glyn Johns ('You Never Cry Like a Lover' and 'Best of My Love' only)
Recorded at Olympic Studios, London; Record Plant Studios, Los Angeles
Record label: Asylum
Release date: March 1974
Highest chart positions: 28 (UK); 17 (US)
Running time: 35:40

In September 1973, the band returned to London to record the third album with Johns, again at Olympic Studios. By this time, the general relationships between band members and producer were starting to fray. Frey and Henley were hankering after a harder rock sound, but Johns still felt their strength lay in the country rock and vocal harmony side, the approach that Leadon still preferred. At one stage, Johns shut down the argument by telling them that The Rolling Stones and The Who were rock bands; Eagles weren't.

Meisner, the quietest and least assertive member, said he wasn't happy with the overall sound they were getting. When Johns asked him to elaborate, he said that every time he heard one of their records on a radio station with poor reception and interference, it didn't sound at all good. Johns thought he was joking, and then found out he really did mean it. Leadon, the main standard-bearer of their more country music-orientated side, was the only one who still got on really well with him.

Another matter that grated on Johns was Frey and Henley's perfectionism, their insistence on polishing their songs and persistently rewriting lyrics. Henley told him that they set the bar very high, insisting that whenever listeners heard what they thought was a bad song on one of their albums, it reflected on all of them. Frey agreed wholeheartedly, explaining that they agonised over every lyric, down to every 'and', 'the' and 'but'. He likened it to building a table, and once it was completed, 'deciding how much time you want to spend sanding and glazing it'.

To add to their woes, the foursome were evidently not getting along so well with each other. It was still a love-hate relationship between them. Henley told Bud Scoppa that they had developed a 'theory of creative tension'. They were all different, they argued and even fought with each other, and they'd never expected to make more than two albums together 'because we found out we didn't get along. But things kept getting better in spite of ourselves.' Even so, Johns found it necessary to remind Frey, in particular, that all four were equally important to the sound of the band. It wasn't what Frey wanted to hear.

To make matters worse, they had arrived with very little new material to work on. About four weeks' work yielded only two really satisfactory tracks, so Johns suggested they take a break, write a few more songs, and return when they were ready. They went home and promptly found a new manager in Irving Azoff, who immediately recommended another producer. Johns felt it was for the best, as they were plainly ill-matched. He knew they would be in better hands with Bill Szymczyk, who had trained as a sonar technician with the US navy, then became a sound engineer and then producer for the likes of B.B. King, The J. Geils Band and Joe Walsh. Szymczyk had the greatest respect for Johns and his work, and took the precaution of contacting him for his approval before stepping into his shoes. Johns gave him his blessing: 'Better you than me, mate!'

Once the band had written and acquired more new songs, they went into Record Plant Studios, Los Angeles. The whole atmosphere proved far more conducive to making the music they wanted, and several more tracks were completed quite swiftly. Matters were made easier by the fact that Szymczyk had the utmost respect for Henley's perfectionism as a lyricist, more so than Johns had done. He said the drummer was always the English Lit. major. 'The final lyrics always seemed to be his. Until he pronounced the words done, they weren't done.'

Yet one further issue was becoming ever more important. For the more rock-orientated style that was within their sights, band and producer realised they needed a more powerful guitarist. Leadon and Frey already knew Don Felder, who was then playing guitar in the David Crosby and Graham Nash Band. He was initially invited as a guest musician to add some 'real dirty slide' to 'Good Day in Hell', and they nailed it together after six takes in the studio. Frey, who sang lead vocal, said afterwards that he sounded like Duane Allman reincarnate, and Felder felt there could be no higher praise. Next, they tried another Frey-led number, 'Already Gone', and again the additional guitar turned a good song into something special. When Felder left the studio, he was convinced it had been just another session until, to his surprise, the next day, Frey rang and invited him to join as a full-time member.

In Britain, where the band was beginning to build a dedicated fan base, Jeff Ward of *Melody Maker* gave the record an ecstatic review. Their third album, he wrote, was 'a little gem ... shows a steadily maturing band playing some unusually evocative, finely-honed music that quite simply is a joy to hear'.

The third album was the only studio one not to feature a photograph of the band on the sleeve, which was printed on a textured surface. Burden suggested that they should feature a painting by Arizona artist Beatien Yazz that he had bought for a pittance on a market stall. When he discovered the artist's name, all he could find in lieu of an address was the fact that he collected his post regularly on the Navajo Native American reservation. Asylum sent him a generous cheque but never heard back whether he received it or not.

'Already Gone' (Jack Tempchin/Robb Strandlund) 4.15

The opening track was one of three songs not written by the band, and Tempchin and Strandlund originally wrote it as a country tune. They played it to Frey, who tried it with the band during the London sessions, gave up on it at first and made another attempt on their return home. He had realised at once that it had the potential to be a great rock song, and when he played the band's studio demo down the phone to the original writers, they were astonished to hear how they had transformed it.

It became one of those powerful, ultra-infectious numbers that burst out of the radio just as forcefully as 'Take It Easy' had almost two summers earlier. Rock 'n' roll guitar goes hand in hand with an irresistibly commercial tune and chorus. It is a break-up song, but a celebratory one, albeit with something of a bitter aftertaste. The narrator has heard on the grapevine that his girl's about to dump him, so he will dump her first and realises he must 'sing this victory song'. It has a slightly vengeful line in the first verse as he warns her, 'you'll have to eat your lunch all by yourself'. Towards the end, he realises that so often 'we live our lives in chains, and we never even know we have the key'. Some people regard it a somewhat distasteful lyric, even demeaning to women – though if she was going to give her man his marching orders anyway, he did, after all, save her the trouble.

Up to the end of the last verse, it sits comfortably on three chords, and then without warning, a modulation in the chorus moves it up three keys from G to C, thus taking the general feeling of exhilaration to a new level. Frey's 'all right, nighty night' – was an ad-lib he threw in at the last moment, saying afterwards, 'that's me being happier, that's me being free'. Part of Frey's *joie de vivre* was as a result of his feeling more comfortable in the studio with a new producer, who showed he would get much better results out of the band if he 'let everyone stretch a bit'.

The first single from the album, in April 1974, it charted at number 32. In Britain, it received regular airplay on release around four months later, thanks largely to Johnnie Walker, the most open-minded of Radio 1's daytime radio presenters at the time. While it missed the Top 50, more importantly, it sent buyers to look for the album instead, resulting in it becoming their first British chart success. Across the Atlantic, they would always be more of an albums band than a singles one (good news for band and record label, in other words, better sales and more credibility with an older audience), more *Old Grey Whistle Test* than *Top of the Pops*. It became the favourite Eagles song of Francis Rossi, front man of Status Quo, who made no secret of his desire to steer his band into a more country rock direction and away from the three-chord, 12-bar boogie with which they were identified so heavily at

---

the time. In an interview on Radio 2 with Walker in 2022, he recalled going to a gig on the *Hotel California* tour, saying he was 'not happy' until they had played 'Already Gone', and thought for a long time that in musical terms they 'could have tried to head somewhere that way'.

'You Never Cry Like a Lover' (J.D. Souther/Henley) 4.00
In the first of two surviving tracks from the London sessions, Don takes vocals on a mournful tune about two lovers between whom the old communication has broken down. 'Your life goes on like a broken down carousel, where somebody left the music on.' Frey adds piano and some soaring melodic guitar solo work and the results are pleasant if not one of their better ballads.

'Midnight Flyer' (Paul Craft) 3.55
Written by the Memphis tunesmith best remembered for the splendidly titled Bobby Bare country hit 'Dropkick Me Jesus (Through the Goalposts of Life)', this was probably the last more or less pure country tune they committed to record, and perhaps indicative of how poorly prepared they had been for the third album. Meisner takes vocal while Leadon plays sterling banjo bluegrass on a brisk 'gotta be travellin' on' song. Just as adventurous bass riffing seems set to take it into a good ol' yeehah hoedown on the fadeout, a pungent guitar solo with mildly psychedelic overtones dominates the last minute or so and moves them demonstrably closer to the rock that they were keen to embrace.

Henley was glad to record something in that vein, as he had always been a fan of bluegrass, and maintained that Leadon was one of the top contemporary banjo players around. Having the song on their album gave them a certain amount of authenticity and credibility, and demonstrated their versatility. It was, however, a double-edged sword as it helped to reinforce their image as a country rock band, something from which they were increasingly keen to escape. The music industry and the media saddled them with that label at the start of their career, he said, and no matter how diverse their musical palate might be, it was impossible to leave that stereotype behind. 'At the end of the day, we're an American band. We're a musical mutt with influences from every genre of American popular music. It's all in there, and it's fairly obvious.'

'My Man' (Leadon) 3.29
Gram Parsons, who had been briefly a member of The Byrds and then a bandmate of Leadon in The Flying Burrito Brothers, died after an overdose of morphine and alcohol in September 1973. Eagles had just arrived in London when they were given the news. As Parsons was the first of Leadon's musical friends to pass away so suddenly, he was shocked and immediately began writing a tribute, which he finished when they returned to Los Angeles. His lyrics refer to a man loved by those who 'knew that his song came from deep

down inside, you could hear it in his voice and see it in his eyes'. As he had not completed the words, Henley suggested he should reference the title of one of Parsons' songs; hence a line about 'that old hickory wind [calling] him home'. A wistful pedal steel guitar and the other members' harmonies accentuate what was probably Leadon's best-ever tune. It was released as the lead track of a maxi-single in Britain in May 1975, with 'Take It Easy' and 'Tequila Sunrise' on the reverse.

Ironically, despite his friendship with Parsons, in an interview not long before his death, the latter was quite disdainful about Eagles' music, calling it 'bubblegum' and saying there was 'too much sugar in it'. Parsons' two solo albums, the second released posthumously, were favourably reviewed at the time but sold poorly. A case of jealousy?

'On the Border' (Henley/Leadon/Frey) 4.23

The title track finds the band attempting to break new ground lyrically and musically. A three-way collaboration, the majority written by Henley, and in his words, it was 'a thinly, perhaps thickly, disguised political piece about Nixon, the trouble he was in'. He added self-deprecatingly that at the time, they 'weren't old and mature enough to make any sense out of it then', and their producer didn't know what to do with it either. (How convenient for them to have a producer to blame if their bold new experiment failed.) They were still learning their craft as songwriters and with hindsight, perhaps thought that as novices in their mid-twenties, they weren't ready to make the portentous political statements in song they really wanted to. Henley said the final result was completely different from how he had envisioned it. He thought it was 'an odd song', with a clash of styles and influences, 'and I'm not sure it ever became what it could have been, musically'.

At the time they wrote and recorded it, an embattled President Richard Nixon (known slightingly as 'Tricky Dicky') was engulfed in the Watergate scandal, which led to his resignation from high office in August 1974 before he could be impeached and dismissed. The affair had led to a general lack of faith in the American government, and widespread concerns about officials exceeding their brief with regard to privacy issues. The band members and commentators then and ever since have variously described it as their effort at an R&B song, something that they would only begin to experiment with seriously on their fourth album, and 'a unique groove somewhere between Sly Stone and Neil Young'. Its main features are Frey's funky guitar riff, background vocals inspired above all by The Temptations, and handclap overdubs in which all the band and others assisted, the producer among them. This explained the sleeve credit to T.N.T.S. or Tanqueray and tonics, Szymczyk's favourite tipple, their aim being to add 'a nice element of spontaneity or anti-perfection', in marked contrast to the meticulous care that they generally applied to their recordings. As it was one of the last songs to be completed for the album and had to be finished to meet a deadline,

Henley resorted to a Black Molly, a truck driver's pill, and stayed up all one night until it was done. Interestingly, Leadon had a hand in its composition, although musically, it is as far removed from his country and bluegrass style as anything they had yet committed to vinyl. That was proof enough, it should be said, that he was as ready as the rest of them to experiment with different musical non-country genres outside his comfort zone.

As for the lyrics, they're open to different interpretations. In the first verse, they're railing against authority and big brother, minding their own business while being told to get on one side or the other. They're out on the border, trying to remain non-aligned or politically neutral, perhaps, refusing to bow to the dictates of law and order. The final line is a blink or you'll miss it valedictory to the president, whose term of office was approaching an involuntary end – 'say goodnight Dick', a catchphrase that had been made famous on *The Smothers' Brothers* TV show, said by Frey or Henley – they couldn't remember which.

Although it was the title track, it remains one of the band's least-known songs, perhaps because it is rather unfocused and never became a favourite with radio programmers. 'On the Border' has always been an elusive work, not to say their oft-overlooked elephant in the room (or the back catalogue). *Classic Rock* later chose it as their 'worst' song on the album. To them, it was 'a clumsy attempt at dunking on recently resigned President Richard Nixon [and not] as sharp as it needs to be lyrically or musically'.

'James Dean' (Jackson Browne/Frey/J.D. Souther/Henley) 3.38
The short life of the 1950s American 'rebel without a cause' was celebrated by many iconic musical figures in one way or another, but this tribute was developed from an idea begun by Browne. The result was not one of their finer moments. A powerhouse of a guitar and drums intro, an insistent bassline throughout, a verse structure that is close to a 12-bar blues in disguise, and the sound of wheels roaring down the highway near the end, are the plus points. It has also been pointed out on online forums that the final note bears a remarkable similarity to the closing chord on The Beatles' 'She Loves You'.

What lets it down is an over-repetitive lyric and some pretty uninspired rhyming – 'James Dean, I know just what you mean, you said it all so clean'. Frey later said that he thought the best line in it was 'I know my life would look all right if I could see it on the silver screen', but it had little competition. It might have passed as the B-side of any 1974 British glam rock single, but the band had already set the bar high and this sounds like something finished off in a hurry to meet the deadline. It had originally been started sometime before, during the *Desperado* sessions, but as it wouldn't have fitted in on that album with its Old West outlaws theme, it was put aside for completion at a later date. The *Melody Maker* piece referred to above singled it out for criticism as the only track about which the reviewer had misgivings, saying that it suffered from several clichés and was not up to the high standard of the rest. It came out as a single in Britain in May 1974 to little attention, and in America three months later, but only reached a paltry number 77.

'Ol' 55' (Tom Waits) 4.21

'Ol' 55' was the opening track on Waits' debut album *Closing Time*, issued in 1973. Geffen played a demo of the song in his office to Frey, who immediately took to it. He loved the idea of recording a song about a car (in the case of this song, a '55 Buick, according to Waits), and the mental picture of driving home at sunrise, thinking about where he had been the previous night. A slow, wistful song almost like a country waltz, Eagles' version followed the mood and tempo of the original, with Al Perkins, former member of Shiloh and then The Flying Burrito Brothers, on pedal steel guitar, and Frey playing piano.

As they were keen to give Waits a higher profile, they invited him to open for them at the Red Rocks Amphitheatre, Colorado, on a show in August 1975, and were annoyed when fans booed him as he took the stage. It didn't prevent him from making public his lack of enthusiasm for them, or what they had done to the song, calling it 'a little antiseptic'. In an interview with *NME* a year later, he said they were 'about as exciting as watching paint dry. Their albums are good for keeping the dust off your turntable and that's about all.'

'Is It True?' (Meisner) 3.14

Meisner's second lead vocal, and only contribution to the album as a writer, this gentle song is the uncomplicated confession of a former 'wild one' who can love his intended better than the one who has taken her for a fool and evidently dumped her. It's an attractive tune, boasting lead guitar throughout, a little reminiscent of George Harrison, although tending towards blandness and hardly the bassist's best. He would, however, make up for it in style with a real jewel of a ballad on the next album.

'Good Day in Hell' (Henley/Frey) 4.25

The song that required a tougher guitar than either Frey or Leadon could supply, and thus brought Felder into the band, is a slow-burning rocker with a hint of Allen Toussaint's 'Play Something Sweet (Brickyard Blues)' in the tune. Boasting both its writers on shared vocals, it was written in part as a tribute to Gram Parsons and also Danny Whitten, a songwriter and former guitarist in Neil Young's Crazy Horse, who had died in 1972 after a drug overdose, though the lyrics can be construed two ways. The devil ensnaring the main character in the song could be either a heroin addiction or a femme fatale.

'Best of My Love' (Henley/Frey/J.D. Souther) 4.34

The second of the tracks recorded in London, this is a deceptively sweet love song that, on closer listening, reveals a lyric musing sadly on a soured relationship, 'coming apart at the seams'. They spent too long in the wrong company, the 'beautiful places and loud empty places ... wasting our time on cheap talk and wine', and now it's make or break time. It was later revealed that Henley had been inspired to write this while breaking up with his girlfriend of the time, Suzannah Martin. A measured rhythm guitar throughout, softly sighing pedal steel guitar, and a more cavernous, echoing bass than usual complement Henley's vocal and the harmonies. He and Frey had been working on it in London, but realised it needed a bridge. A telephone call to Souther in Los Angeles brought him on a transatlantic flight the following day, and he helped them to complete it.

As the album and first two singles had been less successful than expected, they were prepared to swallow their disappointment and begin planning the next record. Frey tried to insist that 'Best' should not be put out as a single, probably on the grounds that it sounded too like 'Desperado'. Souther was told that Asylum had no plans to do so, as they thought it was too long and too slow for a 45. Nevertheless, they overruled his wishes and duly issued it in November 1974. The band were on tour at the time and only too late did they realise that it was not the complete recording but had been faded early and truncated to a playing time of 3.25. Henley threatened to demand its withdrawal from sale, but the label refused, insisting that radio would refuse to play an uncut version.

As if to prove their point, Jim Higgs, a DJ at Station WKMI in Kalamazoo, Michigan, was already playing it repeatedly, and other presenters were starting to follow suit. After a three-month ascent, it gave them not only their second *Billboard* Top 10 single but also their first number one, for one week of March 1975. When it had sold a million copies, Irving Azoff sent a gold record with a piece cut out to the Asylum office, mounted with a caption, 'The Golden Hacksaw Award'. Back in London, Johns felt vindicated, saying it was the record that really established them, after they had turned themselves into what they thought was a rock 'n' roll band, 'a pretty lame one, in my view'.

Forty years later, the band undertook a History Of The Eagles tour, made contact with Higgs (now retired), and invited him and his daughter to one of their shows. Both were invited backstage so the band could thank him in person.

The song also became a single in Britain in January 1975 but failed to spark any interest or sales until it became one half of a double A-side the following year. Yvonne Elliman covered it on her album *Rising Sun* also in 1975 and it became a single in the Netherlands, while Rod Stewart included a version on his album *Still the Same*, in 2006.

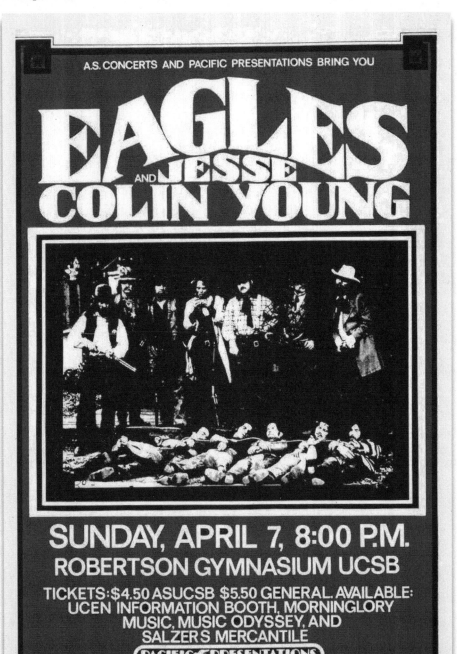

One of These Nights (1975)

Personnel:
Glenn Frey: vocals, guitars, piano, harmonium
Don Henley: vocals, drums, percussion, tabla
Bernie Leadon: vocals, guitars, banjo, mandolin, pedal steel guitar
Randy Meisner: vocals, bass guitar
Don Felder: vocals, lead and slide guitars
Additional musicians:
David Bromberg: fiddles ('Journey of the Sorcerer')
Royal Martian Orchestra: strings ('Journey of the Sorcerer')
Albhy Galuten: synthesiser ('Hollywood Waltz')
Jim Ed Norman: piano ('Lyin' Eyes', 'Take It to the Limit'), orchestrations, string arrangements
Produced and engineered by Bill Szymczyk
Recorded at Criteria Studios, Miami; Record Plant Studios, Los Angeles
Record label: Asylum
Release date: June 1975
Highest chart positions: 8 (UK); 1 (US)
Running time: 43:15

Having started 1975 with a chart-topping single at home, the band were on a roll as they recorded their fourth album, begun during the previous winter. It had been a hectic year for them, as in addition to their own recording and touring commitments, they were also playing on sessions for albums by Jackson Browne, Randy Newman, Linda Ronstadt, Dan Fogelberg, and the guitarist and singer who would soon become an Eagle himself, Joe Walsh. With regard to their own work, Asylum was continually pressing them for a delivery date, to which Frey responded that the first three albums had been the product of 20 years' living, and they could hardly be expected to present them with a fourth in 20 minutes. Henley grumbled that record company pressure was affecting his creativity, and there was limited availability from their two regular writing collaborators, Browne and Souther, who were away for part of the time on tour with the Souther-Hillman-Furay Band. Nevertheless, it would be the first Eagles album on which every track was written partly, if not completely, by at least one member of the band.

At the same time, their problems with Leadon were coming to a head. He was embarking on a healthier lifestyle than the others and his weaning himself off too much drink and drugs led to tension. The same could be said about his relationship with Patti Davis. The daughter of the governor of California and future President Ronald Reagan, with whom she was at odds, she was a liberally minded environmentalist. Despite this common outlook, Henley disliked her and resented Leadon's insistence that she should be allowed to join them in the studio, as John Lennon had with Yoko Ono during the last fractious days of The Beatles. Moreover, Leadon felt increasingly marginalised with the increasing musical shift from country to rock and R&B. Also, like Meisner, he was annoyed that Frey and Henley were excluding them by taking rough mixes away from the studio so they could listen to them on their own, making decisions on what changes needed to be done without consulting the others.

The album was not only their first to top the American charts, which it did for five weeks but also heralded their international breakthrough, particularly in Britain. A few days after release across the Atlantic, they appeared at the midsummer music show at Wembley Stadium, London, on a bill headlined by Elton John and The Beach Boys. They went down a storm, and a few days later, *One of These Nights* entered the album chart in the Top 10, while demand for their back catalogue ensured that the previous two albums appeared not far behind.

The image on the front of the sleeve was a cow skull painted by Boyd Elder, an artist whose work was particularly admired by the band, and who had been one of the associates in the photograph of the back of *Desperado*. Burden chose it as the centrepiece of the design as he said it represented to him 'where the band was coming from and where they were going'.

'One of These Nights' (Henley/Frey) 4.51

The number that Frey later called a 'quantum leap', a 'breakthrough song', and would choose as his favourite out of everything they ever recorded, was ample proof that a pronounced musical shift had taken place, something at which the title track of their previous album had hinted. After the Watergate scandal of the previous year and the subsequent turmoil in Washington, it was a dark time, the mood of America had changed accordingly, and Henley's reaction was to come up with something that, in his own words, would capture the spirit of the times. Looking back years later, he called it their 'satanic country rock period'. How can we write something with that flavour, with that kind of beat, and still have the dangerous guitars?' The lyrics certainly have that sense of danger – and of idealism: 'searching for the daughter of the devil himself, searching for an angel in white, searching for a woman who's a little of both'. When they began recording it, Henley sang a line saying he'd been 'searching for the daughter of God'. Although the others regarded his word as tantamount to law when it came to writing lyrics, they all told him he'd have to change it unless he wanted a bunch of religious zealots putting a price on his head, and he altered it to 'searching for an angel in white'.

Far removed from country, the musical setting reflects their passion for R&B. As their mentor Bob Seger said, it was 'kind of a soul song'. Frey had recently been listening to soul and R&B, from Al Green and Otis Redding, to the more recent Gamble & Huff Philadelphia productions and vocal groups like The Spinners (or Detroit Spinners in the UK, to avoid confusion with the traditional folk group from Liverpool). Another recent favourite of his was Bobby Bland's minor hit of the previous year, whose 'I Wouldn't Treat a Dog (The Way You Treated Me)' bore more than a passing resemblance in structure to 'One of These Nights'. Henley was a great admirer of Al Jackson Jr., the session drummer on several of Willie Mitchell's productions for Al Green and others, where he would hit the snare and the ride tom-tom at the same time on the backbeat.

Frey starts the song with a little minor descending chord progression, while the lyrics come from Henley, who starts singing, 'one of these nights' over the top of it. According to Felder, it was written as an R&B song on acoustic piano, but sounded wrong that way. Meisner was snowed in at his home in Nebraska and unable to reach the studio, so Felder worked out an introduction on bass, recorded it as a demo and taught Meisner the part when he arrived, a job which took almost two days. He was also responsible for the guitar break.

The Barry Gibb-like falsetto vocals towards the end of the song, contributed by Henley and Meisner, were a new innovation for the band. 'The song is a great showcase for high harmony,' Henley commented. 'Meisner hit some notes that only dogs could hear. We also started getting into harmony parts on guitars that simulated horn riffs.' Frey was particularly enthusiastic about Henley's vocals, which allowed them to go in a more soulful direction. Coincidentally, the band were sharing the Criteria Studio with The Bee Gees, who at the time were recording their album *Main Course,* one track of which was 'Jive Talkin'', the song that showed the world that they were capable of far more than the lush, richly orchestrated love songs with which they had become so heavily identified. Henley admitted that the 'four-on-the-floor' bass-drum pattern and vocals on their song were an unashamed 'little nod to disco'. Even more coincidentally, 'Jive Talkin'' was the single that would replace 'One of These Nights' at the summit in America that summer.

As with 'Best of My Love', Asylum edited the album track for its single release, the 3.28 cut removing the first 20 seconds of bass from the intro, and with an earlier fade at the end. Although they disliked the fact that the company used to edit tracks or fade them early for single release in order to keep the radio stations onside, Henley accepted that they were valuable promotion for the album, and there was no point in stopping the practice. He had no time for the argument from Led Zeppelin and others that hit singles were beneath them, damaged album sales and would attract a fickle teen audience who deserted them within a year or two, certainly as far as the British market was concerned. Hit singles were no crime, he said. The view that they couldn't be good for a band from an artistic view was nonsense as far as he was concerned, especially if The Beatles, Bob Dylan and Neil Young had all benefited from them. This was the way the record business was structured, in America at least, 'and if you don't have singles, you can forget it. You could work for ten years making eclectic and artistic underground albums and maybe you'll get the recognition you deserve when you're half dead.'

'Too Many Hands' (Meisner/Felder) 4.43

The first of two songs featuring Meisner on vocal, this is built mainly around a much-repeated chord sequence on acoustic guitar, with Henley's tabla giving it an oriental atmosphere reminiscent of The Beatles' 'Within You, Without You'. Felder and Frey's dual guitar work adds some bite from about halfway through onwards. Despite what reviewers initially thought, the lyric – 'She's one of a kind, sometimes hard to find, she's a rainbow' – is not about a girl who has always been the centre of attention, probably longing to be alone, and whose best days are apparently behind her, but about the human toll on a threatened environment. In a subsequent interview with Steve Clarke of *NME*, Henley pointed out emphatically that the song was about the environment, and that the line 'there's too many hands being laid on her' referred to the planet.

Although it's an interesting variation in style that would have sounded totally out of place on any of the first three albums, musically, it tends to sound stuck in the same groove throughout, with no variation to speak of. Nevertheless, it provides a fine showcase for the vocals of their bassist, who, according to Frey, had really 'found himself' as a vocalist within the last year or so, singing 'with so much brilliance on the record'. He delivered on such high intensity as well; 'he even sounds a little like Gene Pitney.'

'Hollywood Waltz' (Henley/Frey/Bernie and Tom Leadon) 4.04

Leadon was granted two writer's credits on what would be his final album with the band, the first a collaboration with Henley, Frey and also his younger brother Tom, formerly a member of Tom Petty's early band Mudcrutch, and, like most of the other Eagles, one of Linda Ronstadt's backing musicians. Henley took lead vocal on the song that he and Frey had largely rewritten, albeit with a subconscious flavour of the 1940s favourite 'Tennessee Waltz', as recorded by Patti Page, Connie Francis, Leonard Cohen and many others. The lyrics suggest that the subject is not an individual woman but about Southern California, with the 'lovers' being real estate developers and others, who came and exploited the place for profit without putting anything back, leaving it a sadly tarnished shadow of its former self while they moved on to go and destroy or at least diminish somewhere else. This was a theme that Henley would develop one album later in what became one of their finest songs ever.

As the title suggests, it is a charming ballad in waltz time and the perfect vehicle for their vocal harmonies, piano and steel guitar.

'Journey of the Sorcerer' (Leadon) 6.40

Prog rock alert, readers. The longest track the band had yet committed to vinyl, and certainly the most adventurous, was surely Leadon's greatest moment. Much of this instrumental alternates between his slow, measured banjo picking, joined at times by lead guitar and percussion, later intercut with a stirring orchestral theme. There are shades of Jethro Tull and ELO to be heard, culminating in the instruments speeding up during the last minute or so as the drums come in and the banjo sounds more like a sitar. There are elements of raga rock, as explored by the likes of The Beatles, The Rolling Stones and The Move several years earlier. Some critics regard it as tedious filler, but to others, it's nothing of the kind. It's a tantalising glimpse, at the very least, of how the band might have proceeded had the increasingly marginalised Leadon been given more free rein. Henley and Frey disliked it and had to be persuaded to allow it on the album.

One of the track's most fervent admirers was Douglas Adams, creator of *The Hitchhiker's Guide to the Galaxy*, which began life in 1978 as a BBC radio comedy, subsequently becoming a mini-series of books, a television series, several plays, a video game and eventually a film. Adams, who played guitar and piano for fun and was passionate about the music of Pink Floyd, chose 'Journey of the Sorcerer' as the perfect theme music for the radio programme. The original recording was used, but due to publishing and copyright issues, once the TV series, film and other spin-offs were developed, re-recordings by other musicians had to be used.

'Lyin' Eyes' (Frey/Henley) 6.22

Frey and Henley were regular patrons of Dan Tana's restaurant in Los Angeles, which attracted regular custom from other wealthy clientele. One night Frey spotted an attractive young woman there on the arm of a fat, obviously much older man. 'Look at those lyin' eyes,' he remarked to Henley. Bob Buziak, one of the record company executives who sometimes accompanied them on their nights out on the town, later commented that as soon as he said it, 'pens and napkins flew'. From that comment developed the title and also the story of a girl trapped in a loveless relationship, lonely in their 'big old house', finding compensation with her boyfriend – or should it be sugar daddy – in 'the cheatin' side of town'. Later in the song, she discovered that he was not her saviour after all and seeks solace in pouring herself a strong one while she stares out at the stars in the sky, wondering 'how it ever got this crazy'. Once started, the song flowed easily and was completed in a couple of evenings. Frey, who wrote most of the lyrics and sang lead (the only song on the album where he did), said that the story had always been there. Once they began working on it, 'there were no sticking points, lyrics just kept coming out, and that's not always the way songs get written.' The song could have been even longer than that. Frey later said that there were additional verses that weren't used.

Some of the band's former girlfriends were mildly repelled by the misogyny of it all. Frey, Henley and the rest were living beyond the rules, they insisted, with all the fame, drink, drugs, money, good living and above all, glamorous women they could ever possibly want. And still, they had to portray themselves in their music as the victims of the female company they ruthlessly took advantage of and then cast aside. To them, the song should have been named 'Lyin' Guys'.

Leadon, who contributed some tender mandolin in the penultimate verse, thought it was one of their finest achievements. While Henley could sing the phone book and make it sound interesting, he said Frey was a great storyteller. 'Just listen to the way he sings 'Lyin' Eyes'.'

The second verse, the second chorus and four lines from the third verse were edited for the 4.14 single version. In America, it reached number two for two weeks, and like its predecessor, peaked at number 23 in Britain.

'Take It to the Limit' (Meisner/Henley/Frey) 4.48

Eagles wrote and recorded several ballads, but Meisner wrote most of and sang lead on what was perhaps the most achingly beautiful and poignant number in the whole of their catalogue. One night at home, while he was on his own, he started singing, 'All alone at the end of the evening, and the bright lights have faded to blue,' and realised it made a perfect opening line for the next song. It was also, he remarked, partly a commentary on ageing. 'How you keep trying until you've done everything you expected to do, achieved everything you wanted, yet you have to keep going for one more day, keep punching away?' Once Henley and Frey had helped him to complete it and it was ready to record, Szymczyk decided it had something of the feel of Harold Melvin and the Blue Notes' 'If You Don't Know Me by Now', and aimed for that kind of feel in the production, with a little assistance from Norman's piano and string arrangement. The combination of this and Meisner's vulnerable, yearning vocal, create one of those magical moments where everything just falls into place to perfection. Towards the end, he surprised himself when he hit that exceptionally high note on the chorus. Afterwards, he realised, to his dismay, that if it became a hit, he was going to have to perform it onstage and reach that note again every time. Several years of performing live with them had not alleviated his stage fright or his dislike of being in the spotlight, even for one number.

Released as the album's third single, early in 1976, it became the only one in their career on which he sang lead, and also the first A-side without a lead vocal by Henley or Frey. In America, it peaked at number four, and although charting less high than the previous two, it still became their first gold or million-selling record. It would also prove their most successful British 45 to date, peaking at number 12 as a double A-side with 'Best of My Love', although 'Limit' was the one most frequently played on the radio. Whenever they played the Far East, it would be a firm favourite onstage, or as Frey said, 'When Randy would sing it in Japan – it was mass hysteria.'

'Visions' (Felder/Henley) 3.58

As if to prove that Henley and Frey had not altogether eliminated the spirit of democracy from the band, Felder also has a lead vocal on the album for the first and last time. He wasn't particularly confident about his singing voice. He tried really hard, he wrote self-deprecatingly in his memoirs, 'and the fact that Don and Glenn deigned to let me sing it must have meant something', even if it was added to the album at the last minute and he wasn't particularly proud of his efforts. It was the most up-tempo track of the nine on the album, with a lyric that suggests love and lust in equal measure – 'I had some visions of you, if I can't have it all, just a taste will do' – set to a Southern boogie arrangement, with shades of Lynyrd Skynyrd and The Allman Brothers Band. Frey, Henley and Leadon add a few call-and-respond vocals, supplying at one point, 'Play on, El Chingadero, play on'. Only later did he find out that *chingadero* was Spanish for motherfucker.

'After the Thrill is Gone' (Henley/Frey) 3.56

One thing that had drawn the band to working with Szymczyk was that his first major production job had been for B.B. King in 1969 on the classic blues single 'The Thrill is Gone'. This inspired them to write a song that was a kind of sequel, an introspective look at the aftermath. In professional terms, it was a case of expressing their feelings after the initial excitement as a successful band had begun to diminish. In Frey's words, the record was 'a lot of self-examination, hopefully not too much'. 'What can you do when your dreams come true, and it's not quite like you planned?' runs one couplet that encapsulated how they felt now they had made it. While Henley found 'the whole Eagles thing' very exciting at times, by now 'some of the lustre was beginning to wear off. We were combining our personal and professional lives in song.'

Henley wrote and sang the bridges, while Frey wrote most of and took lead vocal on the verses. A slow tempo, ballad rather than blues, provides an ideal atmosphere, with mournful, almost bluesy lead guitar to match.

'I Wish You Peace' (Leadon/Patti Davis) 3.45

Making the most of things while he still was an Eagle, Leadon brought side two of the album to a close with his third contribution. It was a pleasant if a rather treacly little song, on which he insisted that Patti Davis should be given a writer's credit. Although she and Leadon split up not long afterwards, she boasted that she still collected plenty of royalties from a lyric that reads like their attempt to capture the mood of numbers like Carole King's 'You've Got a Friend' – 'And when storms are high and your, your dreams are low, I wish you the strength to let love grow on.' To be fair, it's a pleasant enough way of passing three and a half minutes, but the saccharine strings do it no favours. (Eagles' 'The Long and Winding Road', anyone?)

The other band members disliked it and didn't want it on the album, Henley magnanimously adding that they put it on as a friendly gesture in order to keep the band together. Leadon told the story a little differently. He said he wasn't writing many songs at the time and he wanted that one recorded for the album. He told Henley that if it was passed over, he was going to break his arm. The irony was not lost on him. 'It's absurd, right? The song is "I Wish You Peace", but I'm going break your fuckin' arm if you don't record it.' The drummer capitulated and his arm remained intact, but later, he dismissed it as 'smarmy cocktail music and something we are not proud of'. This was presumably after all the others had realised that the song was actually intended as a farewell message to the rest of them.

Exit Leadon, enter Walsh, and Their Greatest Hits (1971–1975)

During the recording of *One of These Nights*, the writing was on the wall. As Frey later remarked, he was the rock and roller, while Leadon was the folk-acoustic-bluegrass musician. They were increasingly becoming polar opposites, and the latter became more and more disengaged from the others in both a personal and musical sense. Frey commented that they all had a feeling for at least a year, maybe 18 months, that one day he was going to leave. On a couple of occasions, towards the end, he walked out of meetings and sessions without any warning, and did not reappear for a day or more. In December 1975, the management issued an official statement that he had left the band.

In some subsequent interviews, he claimed that to say he had been fired or forced out of Eagles solely because of musical incompatibility was an over-simplification. It implied that he had no interest in rock, blues or anything but country rock. His tastes were as eclectic as anybody else's, he played a Fender Telecaster and a Les Gibson as well as banjo and mandolin, and his enjoyment of rock 'n' roll was evident from the early albums. Yet Henley said that with his bluegrass roots, Leadon had 'never really messed with rock 'n' roll guitar and he never really understood how to get that dirty rock 'n' roll sound. He was just not schooled or programmed in that area.'

Some years later, he opined that their first producer Glyn Johns had been in a position to create a balance between all four members while they were recording the first two albums. After *Desperado*, and the end of their association with Johns, as far as he was concerned, the band became a 'Don Henley and Glenn Frey show'. Their first producer, he emphasised, was 'very adamant' that he and Meisner 'should be pushed forward as well' as their contributions were just as important, so it should not become 'the Glenn and Don show immediately, which is I think what they wanted'. After Johns, 'the whole dynamic changed ... Don and Glenn had written all the hits.' So, it did become the Don and Glenn show.

Almost immediately afterwards, it was announced that guitarist Joe Walsh would be replacing him. Walsh had been on the same bill as them at the London gig in June 1975 and enjoyed a solo career with records also produced by Szymczyk. Frey respected him as being the perfect all-round guitarist with his roots in the blues who could still play in so many different styles, and he was just the right extra musician to come in and toughen up the sound. He had sat in with them onstage before and they had done his classic 'Rocky Mountain Way' as an encore. He was as keen to join as they were to have him as he was tired of being the front man in his own band, having to hire sidemen and make all the decisions himself, felt drained and was sure his solo career was not really going anywhere. This was in contrast to Szymczyk's views; the producer said he felt Walsh's solo career was going very well at the time, and he almost did not want to see him joining a group again. Above all, he knew the other members, had hung out with them a great deal recently and was confident he could relate to them. Around the beginning of 1975, they had told him that Leadon was likely to go sooner or later, to which his response was, 'If it ever happens, give me a call.' Felder would, in future, be multi-tasking not only on guitar but also mandolin, banjo and pedal steel guitar onstage as necessary.

Recruiting Walsh had been partly the idea of Azoff, as for some time, he was encouraging contact between both parties, knowing that Leadon's time with them was running out. He knew that Walsh, long regarded as something of a guitar hero but in need of a steady band, would help to bring them a tougher musical edge. Most of the band were delighted, especially Felder, who felt 'it was good to be able to bounce off somebody who could give back more than you sent out.' Henley took some persuading as he thought that Walsh might be too much of an extrovert and crowd-pleaser onstage, a joker who could upset their delicate balance as a band that had always rated the quality of their music above any attention-grabbing showmanship antics on the part of any one individual. In an interview with *Musician* several years later, he admitted he also had the feeling that Walsh believed he was doing the band a favour, seemed reluctant to be one of them at first, 'and I think he was almost ashamed of it for a while'.

On the contrary, during some of the first gigs, critics thought he was holding back, as if not altogether comfortable in his new environment, letting Felder be the guitar star instead. Nevertheless, he gradually warmed to his new role, and everyone realised he was giving their sound more fire. The inclusion of 'Rocky Mountain Way' and another of his best numbers, 'Turn to Stone', gave the stage show some additional sparks.

In February 1976, Elektra-Asylum released the first of what would be several compilation albums, *Their Greatest Hits (1971–1975)*. Some music business observers thought the company might be afraid the band had peaked or, worse still, suddenly disband once the personnel began to alter, and intended to strike while they were still hot. At any rate, the suits were impatient for more product in the stores as a stop-gap if nothing else, and as the band seemed in no hurry to begin recording anything new, a compilation would be easy to put together in a short space of time and incur less expense than a brand new collection. Henley was unenthusiastic, complaining that he was not a fan of greatest hits albums and thought it was merely a ploy by the company to get free sales. All the label was worried about, he said, were their quarterly reports, and 'they just wanted product'. He had a point, but like the others, he was surely not averse to receiving a sudden spike in royalties without having to set foot inside the studio in a hurry. Nor was Frey, though he was astonished at its success, as a fair number of buyers probably owned at least some of the previous albums. They received a few hate letters after the record came out, accusing them of selling out, but as they said, there was no way they could stop Asylum from doing what they wanted.

Azoff, who was partly behind the idea, put it more succinctly. They decided it was time for the first greatest hits album, 'because we had enough hits'. Henley eventually became reconciled to the idea, conceding that at least it had bought them some breathing space to work on the forthcoming magnum opus, *Hotel California*. Moreover, it marked the end of an era for them instead of being their epitaph. It opened up the beginning of a new era.

Featuring all previously released material, the front of the sleeve featured an embossed design by Boyd Elder, based on a painted plastic cast of an eagle skull, for which he received a one-off payment of $5,000. The back featured only the tracklisting, with no line-up details or pictures of the band, suggesting that it had been thrown together with some haste. It was certified platinum for one million sales within a week and stayed on the *Billboard* Top 200 for two and a half years, with five non-consecutive weeks at number one and peaking in Britain one place lower. Despite subsequent Eagles compilations during the next four decades and the unreliability of comparable (or accurate) industry sales figures, by 2020, it had sold an estimated 40–45 million copies worldwide, and according to the RIAA (Recording Industry Association of America), 38 million of those had been bought in its own territory, four million more than Michael Jackson's *Thriller,* which had overtaken it in the 1990s but was subsequently relegated to second place. Number three on the list, with 34 million sales in America, would be the next Eagles project – *Hotel California.*

The release of the compilation coincided with the end of EMI's licensing deal in Britain for the Asylum label and a changeover to WEA (Warner Elektra Atlantic). The UK double A-side, 'Take It to the Limit' and 'Best of My Love', which neatly coincided with the album, would be followed around six months later in Britain by three singles released more or less simultaneously, 'Peaceful Easy Feeling' / 'Ol' 55', 'Take It Easy' / 'Witchy Woman', and 'Tequila Sunrise' / 'On the Border'. One can only assume that they were put out largely to keep the band's name in the public eye, with little expectation of chart success, until the next new product was ready.

Hotel California (1976)

Personnel:
Glenn Frey: vocals, guitars, keyboard
Don Henley: vocals, drums, percussion, synthesiser
Joe Walsh: vocals, guitars, keyboards
Randy Meisner: vocals, bass guitar
Don Felder: vocals, guitars, pedal steel guitar
Produced and engineered by Bill Szymczyk
Recorded at Criteria Studios, Miami; Record Plant Studios, Los Angeles
Record label: Asylum
Release date: December 1976
Highest chart positions: 2 (UK); 1 (US)
Running time: 43:28

During the first few weeks of 1976, the band played a few dates in Japan, Australia and New Zealand. In March, they began recording and writing the next album, with regular breaks between April and December, during which there were about 50 concerts in America. Although they had wanted to make the record at Los Angeles, Szymczyk insisted that they went to Florida instead. Ostensibly his reason for getting out of Los Angeles was because he feared an imminent earthquake, but he later revealed that he was desperate to get them out of LA, with all the hangers-on, subsequent partying and no work done.

Over a few days in June, Black Sabbath were also recording their album *Technical Ecstasy* in an adjacent studio at Criteria next door, and they were so loud that Eagles were fed up with having to re-record material and had no choice but to stop several times. Some overdubbing needed to be done later at the Record Plant in Los Angeles. Nevertheless, the album was completed by the autumn. It was a remarkable workload for them all, as Frey, Henley and Walsh had also found time to play on Souther's new solo album *Black Rose*, and as individuals, they also contributed to new releases from Jackson Browne, Rod Stewart, Carly Simon, Linda Ronstadt and Warren Zevon. They were so omnipresent on the local session scene that Radio 1's John Peel quipped how if you were recording in the area, you were advised to lock the studio doors, otherwise, the Eagles would suddenly burst in with a cry of 'Hey guys, making a new album? Let's come and play on it for you.'

Some of their time spent together on making *Hotel California* proved difficult. Leadon's departure had done nothing to improve the general working relationship. Frey and Walsh had bonded well, but Henley did not immediately warm to their new guitarist. He considered Felder far better than Leadon and much more suited to their sound in moving them away from the country rock band tag that they were intent on escaping, but a gulf was growing between Frey and Felder. It was ironic as the former was the one who had personally contacted the latter in the first place and asked him to join as a full-time member. Yet Henley suspected that the outgoing Walsh, who had a more pronounced sense of showmanship onstage, might not fully suit the role.

At the same time, Meisner, a more introverted character whose marriage was about to end in divorce, was increasingly unhappy with Frey and Henley's domination of the band and both of them marginalising him as a contributor to the writing process, leaving him as the sole writer of one song and a contributor to none of the others on the new album. He was also weary of Henley and Frey recording the album on their schedule instead of everybody else's, with the other three getting so tired as they worked into the small hours of the morning that they didn't care about the end result. 'We would have done a track 80 times,' he said, 'and we'd all be looking at ourselves and saying, 'Do you think that's a good one?'' Walsh agreed, saying that it had got to the point where they hated it because they had been working on it for so long. 'It was all we heard for almost a year.'

Rather like *Desperado* (and perhaps like The Beatles' *Sergeant Pepper*), the record became a concept album in a fairly non-specific way, with an underlying commentary about the band's view of the music business. According to Frey, 'The Hotel was a metaphor for the myth-making of Southern California and the American dream. There's a fine line between the dream and a nightmare.' As with *Desperado*, they did not start with the idea of any specific theme running throughout the record. However, having completed 'Life in the Fast Lane' and begun work on 'Hotel California' and 'New Kid In Town' with Souther, they felt they were 'heading down a long and twisted corridor and just stayed with it with songs from the dark side, looking at the seamy underbelly of L.A. – the flip side of fame and failure, love and money'.

The photograph for the front of the sleeve turned into quite a convoluted saga. To complete it, their new art director John Kosh and photographer, David Alexander, had to sit precariously on the top of a 60-foot cherry picker dangling over Sunset Boulevard as they worked at sunset, trying to capture the brightly lit Beverly Hills Hotel into something vaguely sinister, so it would match the tone of the album itself. They succeeded in modifying the image once it was taken but not in concealing its identity. Once the owners realised it was their property, they threatened Kosh with a 'cease and desist' action, something that might have required Asylum to withdraw the record and issue it with a new design altogether. Fortunately, his attorney managed to placate the hotel management by pointing out that the album's release had benefited their business as well, with their requests for bookings increasing threefold once the word got out.

Additional information and other material included in the sleeve design on vinyl and subsequent issues on cassette, CD and other media varied from country to country. In some cases, alongside individual track credits, they also included the full lyrics to the title track. Unlike many of their contemporaries, they were not in the habit of supplying lyrics in the packaging.

'Hotel California' (Henley/Frey/Felder) 6.30

The title track had its origins in a demo that Felder had recorded in a four-track studio in his spare bedroom at home. The man who had initially impressed them as another Duane Allman could play in more or less any genre, and was therefore not only the perfect foil for Walsh to bounce ideas off and vice versa, but also the very musician they needed to help take them further away from the country rock tag they were still lumbered with, rather against their will. Felder loved working on his own, creating, playing and overdubbing instrumental pieces with six- and 12-string guitars and drum machine. When they were planning the next album, he submitted a series of them on cassettes to 'the gods', his nickname for Henley and Frey. The latter took a cursory listen with obvious lack of interest, but one immediately took his fancy. Felder had used several acoustic and electric guitars set it to a reggae beat and added two solos complementing each other at the end. When he had completed it, he knew he had hit on something special, but it was quite different from anything they had done before and wasn't sure whether it would be appropriate for them.

Much to his delight, the ever-hard-to-please Henley said he loved it, thought it sounded slightly Spanish, and referred to it as 'Mexican Bolero', or 'Mexican Reggae'. As they played around with it and took it in different directions, the original working title was changed to 'Hotel California', as the idea evolved of a lyric about the fantasy of California. It began with a man driving down a desert highway at night in a convertible, seeing the shimmering lights of Los Angeles on the distant horizon. From there, his narrative took on a life of its own, with the man seeing a hotel in the distance and deciding to spend the night there. Once he had stopped in the place and he was served pink champagne under mirrored ceilings, a woman walked in and he decided it was a lovely place that could be heaven or hell. Mission bells began to ring, as the alluring woman lit a candle and led the traveller down a long corridor.

The song took several weeks to complete, from Henley fleshing out his initial inspirations into a finished lyric, working out a reggae-style beat on the drums, to Felder teaching Meisner the bass part he had devised, and Walsh adding his own guitar solo to complement the original one. Szymczyk noted that there were 33 edits in the song, and the coda of Walsh and Felder's guitars at the end of the track took three days alone, Henley insisting that no jamming was allowed and every note had to be just right.

It was their most ambitious creation to date and also the one that has been most interpreted (or misinterpreted, as Henley would have it) by others. At regular intervals over the years, interviewers asked him what the lyrics meant. He would answer with varying degrees of patience that almost every critic had got it wrong, especially the Christian fundamentalists who thought it was merely satanic, and that Hotel California was actually an old church that had been taken over by devil-worshippers. It was not about life in California, he claimed, or even in any specific location, but rather a symbolic piece about

America in general, which he called a land of excess. It could be taken just as much as their interpretation of the high life in Los Angeles, or at the same time as a sweeping portrayal of the dark side of the American dream. To him, it was a way of dealing with 'traditional or classical themes of conflict: darkness and light, good and evil, youth and age, the spiritual versus the secular. I guess you could say it's a song about the loss of innocence or a story about the journey from innocence to experience.'

At the same time, he intended it as a look at contemporary American culture. By calling one song 'Hotel California', he was merely using the state of California as a microcosm for the rest of America and for the self-indulgence of the entire national culture. 'Things simply happen out here or in New York first, whether it's with drugs or fashion or artistic movements or economic trends and then work their way towards the middle of America, he said. 'And that's what I was trying to get at.' He gave short shrift to journalist John Soeder in *Cleveland Plain Dealer* in 2009 when reminded that wine wasn't a spirit, as one line in the song implied. Having sarcastically thanked Soeder for the tutorial, Henley told him he was not the first to misinterpret his words. That line had little or nothing to do with alcoholic beverages but was 'a sociopolitical statement', and he declined to explain it in detail, as it would defeat the purpose of using literary devices in songwriting 'and lower the discussion to some silly and irrelevant argument about chemical processes'.

Nevertheless, imagination continued to run amok as to hidden meanings. Hotel California, said some, was surely a euphemism for drugs. (Although he was no stranger to such an indulgence, Frey once said it was 'anti-excess cocaine'.) The line 'warm smell of colitas' was believed to be either sexual slang, cocaine or marijuana. It was left to Felder to point out that colitas was a plant growing in the Californian desert that bloomed at night and gave off a pungent odour. When they wrote lyrics, Felder (whose rare contributions as a collaborator were musical rather than those of a wordsmith) pointed out that their objective was to do so in such a way that created an atmosphere through touching multiple senses, things that listeners could see, hear, smell and taste. Other observers thought the hotel was a psychiatric hospital, hence the hapless traveller who had stopped for the night and was eventually told he could never leave. Others suggested it was an inn run by cannibals, or the renowned Playboy Mansion, or even a metaphor for the mansion in Scotland that had once been owned by the notorious Aleister Crowley.

Henley must have sometimes wondered what he'd started. Though he remained tight-lipped on the subject, some of the lines were about Loree Rodkin, a professional jewellery designer who had formerly been the fiancée of Elton John's lyricist Bernie Taupin. She then had a brief but intense affair with the drummer before leaving him and returning to Taupin. Her mind, according to the lyrics, was 'Tiffany twisted', and she had the Mercedes-Benz, while she 'entertained the pretty boys that she calls friends' as they danced in the courtyard. A mutual friend said that not only that song but several others

on the album had subtle, indirect references about what he went through
after they had broken up as a couple.

Frey was prepared to shut down all debate by saying that the song was just
like a little movie. 'A lot of it doesn't have to make sense.' He had also had a
certain amount of lyrical input into the work, and said he loved the imagery
that they were using, whether it was in-jokes, mild flights of surreal wordplay or
surreal allusions to a journey from 'shimmering light'. They liked and admired
the way that Steely Dan could say anything in their songs. Walter Becker and
Donald Fagen referred to Eagles in 'Everything You Did' on their previous
album, *The Royal Scam* – 'Turn up the Eagles, the neighbours are listening'. Frey
said that he was told Becker's girlfriend was a huge fan of Eagles and played
them all the time until it drove him mad. Yet between both acts, there was a
friendly rivalry rather than animosity, especially as Eagles greatly respected
Steely Dan, and moreover, Irving Azoff was the manager of both. So Henley and
Frey decided to incorporate a reciprocal reference, hence the line, 'They stab
it with their steely knives, but they just can't kill the beast.' Within three years,
there would be yet another common factor between them. Timothy B. Schmit,
bass guitarist with Poco, sang backing vocals on *The Royal Scam* and a couple
of other Dan albums. Before long, he, too, would be an Eagle.

The band were braced for possible trouble ahead when it was pointed
out that the chord progression of the verses sounded remarkably similar to
'We Used to Know', a track on Jethro Tull's second album *Stand Up* in 1969.
Eagles had been Tull's support band on an American tour of 1972. Felder,
who was largely responsible for the melody, had yet to join, although as a
friend of Leadon, he might have been at one or more of the shows. He denied
having heard Tull's song before and claimed to know little about the band.
Fortunately for them, their leader Ian Anderson accepted that in popular
music, different songs sometimes used the same chord sequence, the number
of chords and different permutations of same not being infinite. As he said,
it was merely the same chord sequence, but in a different time signature,
different key, different context. They probably heard them play the song
onstage as it was part of the set back then 'and maybe it was just something
they kind of picked up on subconsciously'. These things happen. It didn't stop
him from praising it warmly: 'It's a very, very fine song that they wrote, so I
can't feel anything other than a sense of happiness for their sake.' Plagiarism
was the last thing that crossed his mind, although he did 'sometimes allude, in
a joking way, to accepting it as a kind of tribute'. He told Songfacts.com that
the two bands didn't interact much on tour 'because they were countrified
laidback polite rock, and we were a bit wacky and English'.

It stopped around the middle and started again, had a 90-second guitar solo
at the end, and was over six minutes long. The structure broke one of the
golden rules of songwriting, the lyrics ending not with a final chorus but with
that disturbing, open-ended couplet, 'You can check out any time you like,
but you can never leave.' Henley immediately decided it was going to be the

single, and everyone else looked at him in disbelief. While they agreed that the result was absolutely stunning, in their view, it was too slow, much too lengthy and radio stations were unlikely to touch it.

Asylum agreed it sounded like a hit and planned to release it as the second single from the album, but initially, they wanted a shorter version. As they had issued edits of the three hits from *One of These Nights*, they could have removed part of the guitar intro, or faded it earlier without consultation (which might have been a necessary evil or sacrilege by any other name). However, the band were now premier league which entitled them to a greater say in how their work was presented to the public. Henley told them that it would come out as a 45 as it was in all its glory – or not at all. To support his argument, he cited Bob Dylan's *Like a Rolling Stone*, the six-minute mould-breaker in 1965 that became and always remained his highest charting single on both sides of the Atlantic. He could also have named Queen's 'Bohemian Rhapsody', the six-minute epic of a year earlier, that EMI in London once insisted would never be a hit. Asylum gave in and he was vindicated when the almost-complete opus (6.10 according to the label, thus losing 20 seconds) reached the top at home in May 1977 and became their only British Top 10 hit, peaking at number eight.

After the album and the hit single, there was even talk of a *Hotel California* movie. Producer Julia Phillips, whose recent successes in the motion picture industry had included *The Sting* and *Close Encounters of the Third Kind*, contacted Azoff to discuss the possibility and after a meeting with him that sounded like there might be potential, arranged a second one with the manager, Henley and Frey. They came across to her as 'scruffy and sullen', and there were potential difficulties because of an unresolved copyright issue regarding the album involving Geffen and Warner Bros. But the main sticking point was that the songwriters didn't trust the film business or those who worked in it, and Henley knew he'd have no control over such a venture. As one friend put it, he didn't want to see what he regarded as 'his finest, most personal work reduced to the level of a sitcom'.

'New Kid in Town' (Henley/Frey/J.D. Souther) 5.04

It had long been apparent that Eagles were moving further away from country rock mode. Around the time the album was released, Henley told Chris Charlesworth of *Melody Maker* that they were not changing direction, as they were keeping the best of the old style and not abandoning country rock, but just wanted to 'stretch things out a little bit'. They were getting more into R&B, a process they had begun on the third album and been developing ever since. Yet the song that would be *Hotel California*'s first 45 proved that they still had one foot in the genre that originally brought them together. Souther had started it and written a chorus, brought what he had done so far to Frey's house one day and played it to them. Everybody immediately looked at him and told him that was definitely a single. When he said he didn't know what else to do with it, Frey and then Henley fleshed it out with a few more ideas, words and music. Frey called it 'a ham and eggs deal', a three-man song in which they all had a hand in providing lyrics and chords.

The song itself could be interpreted in several ways. Henley said it was about the fleeting nature of love and romance (even if he did not mention his former lover Rodkin by name), and also about the transitoriness of fame, especially in the notoriously fickle music business. Souther endorsed this, adding that they were all approaching the age of 30 and could see that 'the rearview mirror was full of newcomers as hungry as we had been.' He went on that his lyrics had been inspired partly by their fascination with gunfire as an analogy. At some point, he said, 'some kid would come riding into town that was much faster than you and he'd say so, and then he'd prove it.' They were just writing about the young generation – or the young guns – who would replace them before they knew it. Bruce Springsteen, who was destined to become the most important as well as successful American singer-songwriter and performer since Bob Dylan, was currently the musical name to watch, and some thought that he must be the 'new kid in town' they were singing about. Souther denied this, suggesting that if anybody was the subject of the song, it was Bernie Taupin, to whom Don Henley's former lover had recently returned. But by and large, it was about them 'chronicling our own demise, basically saying, "Look, we know we're red hot now, but we also know that somebody's going to come along and replace us – both in music and in love."'

Frey later remarked that Eagles had been around for a good four years, and felt they had done pretty well – but in the music business, there was always competition from the younger generation. They were great admirers of Daryl Hall and John Oates, who were also competing for their market. Were they the new kids in town who could replace them overnight while their backs were turned?

To Eagles biographer Marc Eliot, it was a song largely about the insecurity and heartbreak of any man who had been through the negative experiences of any young man who realised that the woman who he had built his world around had left him and moved on.

Musically, it's a tender, gentle number, with gentle keyboards providing some of the instrumentation that in Leadon's days would probably have been played on steel guitar. Lead guitar soloing is kept to a restrained minimum, with vocal harmonies as ever adding a sweetness to the implied bitterness in the lyrics. Frey handles lead vocal adroitly, especially after the bridge in the song when the key moves up from the key of E in the earlier verses to G for the last one. Meisner plays a *guitarrón*, an acoustic bass, given to him by a friend from Mexico. The song's exquisite vocal harmonies won a Grammy for Best Vocal Arrangement.

The song was released as the first single from the album, but faded early to lose the last 15 seconds of the full version. It gave the band their third chart-topper in America for one week in February and peaked at number 20 in Britain.

'Life in the Fast Lane' (Henley/Frey/Walsh) 4.46

Frey was on his way to a game of poker one evening, being driven by a friend known as 'the Count', because his counting was so terrible. Without any warning, he moved over to the left lane at about 90 miles per hour. Frey told him to slow down, to which he replied, 'Hey, man, it's life in the fast lane.' Frey instantly recognised a new song title.

It's more than a song about leading life at full speed ahead. The lyrics provide a double meaning, a reflection on contemporary privileged lifestyle and the negative side. Frey and Henley devised the tale of an obscenely rich and miserable couple living the life of decadence, who 'had everything and did everything, and lost the meaning of everything', and were bored with the excesses that had become second nature to them. He thought the line that encapsulated them more than any other was 'We've been up and down this highway, haven't seen a goddamn thing.' It summarised their journey; they'd got everything they wanted, and yet they were living in a spiritual ghetto.

In a sense, it was almost a case of 'physician, heal thyself'. Henley later admitted that it was partly about him and the cocaine habit he had developed. He was high for much of the time that they were writing and recording it, and he was attempting to put across the message that coke made people ill. It was turning on him, hurting his back muscles and stomach, and making him paranoid and bad-tempered. What he might have added was that it was another song about themselves as a band that had striven for success, become the top-selling band in America, wealthy beyond their wildest dreams – and where did they go now? Maybe he had to live through the negative side to write about it with authenticity. As ever, the lyrics were a joint effort. Frey and Henley said they had a kind of telepathy going on while they were writing together, and always finishing each other's sentences.

The result is one of the most distinctive tracks on their best, most successful album. The further magic ingredient came at a rehearsal when Walsh was tuning his guitar and bounced off a distinctive riff that came to him on the spur of the moment. They all seized on it at once, made him play it again and taped it. That became the intro, and everything else soon fell into place on probably the funkiest thing they ever recorded, with an insistent bass and drums pattern, and Felder adding a complementary guitar lick to answer Walsh's riff. Both guitars and bass vie for honours on the lead break, and after the final chorus, the title line is repeated a couple of times with some clever use of phasing before the last minute takes off on another dual guitar solo until fade. From then on, Walsh used it regularly as a warm-up exercise before starting recording sessions.

The track became the third single from the album that summer but fell short of the success of the other two. In America, it stalled at 11, while in Britain, generous airplay couldn't lift it into the Top 50, perhaps as so many fans had already bought the parent long player. Radio One presenter Dave Lee Travis used the phased title line as the basis for a jingle on his weekday show for a while.

'Wasted Time' (Henley/Frey) 4.55

By general agreement, this was one of Henley's best-ever vocals. At the time, they were listening especially to Teddy Pendergrass, The (Detroit) Spinners, and the Philadelphia soul singers, and decided they wanted to come up with a production in similar mode. Piano and strings are foremost in the arrangement, with only a light touch from the rhythm section and guitar.

Frey called it 'a Philly-soul torch song', and Henley their own Teddy Pendergrass; 'he could stand out there all alone and just wail.' A big Philly-type production with strings, 'definitely not country rock', he said, was not something to be found on a Crosby, Stills & Nash or Beach Boys record. Henley's singing abilities stretched so many of their boundaries, and Jim Ed Norman, who wrote all their string charts, 'was right there with us in terms of wanting to do something like Thom Bell'.

The subject matter deals with the end of an affair, both partners having walked away from each other, trying to be philosophical about their loneliness as they move on. In the final verse, they conclude that some day they will realise that 'it wasn't really wasted time'. The song was largely Henley's creation, inspired by his breaking up with Loree Rodkin. She was reportedly not flattered by the implication that their liaison had been a waste of time, despite the twist at the end.

'Wasted Time [reprise]' (Henley/Frey/Jim Ed Norman) 1.22

As the band had decided that this was going to be a concept album, they decided that side two would continue where they had left off, hence a short instrumental reprise of the previous track.

'Victim of Love' (Henley/Frey/Felder/J.D. Souther) 4.11

One of the recordings Felder had made at home was an instrumental, tentatively named 'Iron Lung'. He called it thus as the sound evoked a patient wheezing in a hospital ward, and reminded him of a childhood illness. Henley and Frey were both very impressed with it, and one night all three, plus Souther, were at Frey's house, talking about relationships, broken hearts and lost dreams. Felder often wondered if they were in the habit of breaking off relationships with their girlfriends, simply in the interest of retaining that keen emotional edge as songwriters. When Souther commented that having a broken heart was like being the victim of a car crash, Felder agreed that victim was the right word. 'Victim of what?' he asked. 'Victim of love,' Henley responded. Another song title.

Once the four of them had the lyrics complete, Felder assumed he would be singing it. He and Henley sang separate versions in the studio, one after the other, but it was obvious to all of them who was the better vocalist. Felder was the first to admit it, although 'deep down, I wasn't thrilled at losing my slot.' Nevertheless, he makes up for it by adding some impassioned guitar. Unusually they recorded it live in the studio with no instrumental overdubs, merely adding the lead and harmony vocals later, hence the inscription scratched on the run-out-groove of the early vinyl pressing, 'V.O.L. is five piece live'. Frey later said that for a band that did a lot of overdubbing and editing, it was the right thing to do, especially as an answer to the critics who accused them of being over-clinical in the studio. 'We just said, "Look, let's just cut this thing live and this will be it. It'll be what it is."'

'Pretty Maids All in a Row' (Walsh/Joe Vitale) 4.05

Walsh's main contribution to the album was an introspective ballad in waltz time, co-written with Joe Vitale. Vitale had played drums in Walsh's previous band, Barnstorm and would subsequently join Eagles' touring band, freeing Henley up to concentrate properly on vocals for some numbers. Walsh had lyrics for a couple of verses as well as the musical idea but needed additional input. It was completed in the same way as the Frey-Henley collaborations, with both musicians spending a couple of hours together as they came up with ideas simultaneously over their instruments, making minor alterations to verses and chorus until the song was complete.

A bluesy slide guitar break comes about halfway through, but otherwise, the main instruments are Walsh's piano and orchestral-sounding synthesiser. He called it a melancholy reflection on his life to date, and 'a statement that would be valid for people from our generation on life so far'. It was his intention to write something that reflected his love of The Beach Boys, and the final minute of the song is a wordless vocal harmony passage that evokes the sound of the Wilson brothers.

The ultimate accolade was to come much later. In an interview with *The New York Times* in 2020 to coincide with the release of his album *Rough and Rowdy Ways*, including lyrics that namechecked Henley and Frey, Bob Dylan spoke of his love for Eagles' music. He cited 'New Kid in Town' and 'Life in the Fast Lane' as being among his favourites, adding that 'Pretty Maids All in a Row' 'could be one of the best songs ever'. Vitale was thrilled. 'Coming from Bob Dylan, it doesn't get any better than that,' he said.

'Try and Love Again' (Randy Meisner) 5.10

Like Leadon before him, Meisner was becoming increasingly a lone wolf in the band. He seemed unable to handle the stardom factor, the drink and drugs, his health was suffering, and he was going through a divorce. Under pressure to write something for the album, he was sitting at home one evening and the idea suddenly came to him. Like so many of the other numbers on the album, there are two meanings or themes – the approaching end of his marriage and of his relationship with the band. This slow-paced tune has something of the atmosphere of 'Take It to the Limit', though with a more dominant guitar figure and without the rich orchestration.

'The Last Resort' (Henley/Frey) 7.25

The album begins with one of the band's towering achievements and ends with another, a powerful, majestic number that takes several listens to absorb to the full and be appreciated in all its glory. Frey said that they began work on 'Resort' at an early stage in the album and completed it seven months later. 'I called it Henley's opus. I helped describe what the song was going to be about and assisted with the arrangement, but it was Don's lyrics and basic chord progression.' It was the song they would subsequently call light-heartedly 'The Vast Report'. In an interview in 1988 with BBC presenter Roger Scott for a Radio 1 documentary on the album, Frey opined that it was Henley's 'greatest lyrical achievement to this day', and 'probably one of the biggest pieces of musical literature' they had ever tackled, as well as 'slightly depressing, but a classic'. Depressing? – well, sombre, certainly. A classic? – absolutely. Their best song ever, bar none? That's a matter of opinion, but it would receive yours truly's vote without a doubt.

The theme is Henley's searing view of environmental degradation and slaughter in the name of progress. About two years earlier, they played a couple of benefit concerts as support to Neil Young for the Chumash tribe, Native American people indigenous to California. It led to their befriending an elder in the Samu tribe, and they were subsequently invited to attend some of their tribal rituals and drum ceremonies. Their objective was to raise funds for an educational programme that would fully inform the younger members of the tribe about their language and culture. The old man was afraid that the white man's culture was robbing his people of their true identity, annihilating the memory of their time-honoured language, ceremonies and, above all, their pride in their heritage. Their understanding and newly acquired knowledge of the issue made them, Henley in particular, keen to do something to help.

Not long afterwards, he began reading extensively about the raping and pillaging of the land by mining, timber, oil and cattle interests. 'But I was interested in an even larger scope for the song,' he said, 'so I tried to go "Michener" with it.' He vividly recalled going out to Malibu, standing on Zuma beach as he looked out across the ocean, thinking to himself that it was about as far west, apart from Alaska, as anyone could travel on the continent. It was the point where manifest destiny ended – 'right here in the middle of all these surfboards and volleyball nets and motor homes'. Why, he asked, when mankind found something good, did they promptly go and destroy it by their mere presence – 'by the very fact that man is the only animal on earth that is capable of destroying his environment'? From it developed his masterpiece, in which he bared his soul at the destruction of the beauty and spirituality of the world around them, all in the name of civilisation or progress. The result is a masterfully composed diatribe about the desecration of the environment and how people initially revelled in it for their own financial gain, and those who came afterwards either followed suit or chose to look the other way and ignore it.

To illustrate the theme, he and Frey had the idea of a girl from Providence, Rhode Island. Some listeners point to a double meaning here, a religious one, in that Providence might also mean the will of God and not just the place. Her father came from Europe to America, to Providence, but there's nothing left for her there, so she wants to move on, going west on an epic journey in pursuit of the American Dream, where people are smiling. They all speak about 'the Red Man's ways', and how they love the land as they foresee a new virtual paradise and crowd, which they proceed to destroy, through mining and logging activities on a major scale as they lay the mountains low while their towns grow high. Instead of staying to clear up after them, they go into the towns afterwards to celebrate the end of the week's work, or maybe drown their sorrows in drink and drugs, ignoring the havoc their activities were having on the natural world. At this point, the girl seems to disappear, while everyone else crosses the desert and settles in California in search of another paradise where they do the same again, 'hungry for power, to light their neon way and give them things to do'. Power has a double meaning – electricity, bringing with it pollution and blackouts, as well as domination over those around them. Their arrival emphasises the irony in the contrast between the soon-to-be spoiled glory of the Pacific sunset and their insatiable quest for money, sex and fame.

Seven years earlier, Joni Mitchell had sung in 'Big Yellow Taxi', one of the first eco-hits that 'they paved paradise and put up a parking lot'. Henley expresses it in more uncompromising terms; 'Some rich man came and raped the land, nobody caught 'em, put up a bunch of ugly boxes and, Jesus, people bought 'em.' They call it paradise as, for them, it's a comfortable place to live with all mod cons, while they watch the hazy sunset, a symbol of death or at least the end of an era. Pollution is doubtless partly, if not wholly responsible for the haze. The final destination in their journey is Hawaii, the last resort, or final frontier of what they called paradise. But Lahaina is no longer virgin paradise. The 'missionaries' destroyed it years before when they 'brought the white man's burden' there, justifying themselves with a neon sign saying 'Jesus is coming', as they impose their culture and, in the process, destroy what was natural and beautiful about the place.

With each verse, Henley rails ever more fiercely against what they see going on around them. *Homo sapiens* has reached the ocean and there is no more new frontier, no unspoiled place left to go, 'we have got to make it here' as he satisfies his insatiable needs, justifying his trail of destruction 'in the name of destiny and in the name of God'. All he can do is watch the sun go down and kiss paradise goodbye, while he and his fellow members of the wrecking crew, the good Christians in church every Sunday, take a rest from their carnage and sing about how wonderful it will be when they get to heaven. The irony is that they have destroyed all the places they called paradise, in favour of a man-made one that is basically a monument to greed. Virgin land has been developed or rather destroyed in the name of financial gain, masquerading as 'progress' by money-mad people who celebrate afterwards in the crowded bars.

As the co-writer of the song, Frey was in full agreement. One of the song's major themes, he said, was that man kept on creating what he'd been trying to escape – violence, chaos, destruction.

> We migrated to the East Coast, killed a bunch of Indians, and just completely screwed that place up. Then we just kept moving West: move those teepees, we got some train tracks coming through here. Get outta the way, boy!

Ever the perfectionist, Henley remained slightly dissatisfied with the final recorded result, maintaining that, in his opinion, it was never fully realised but 'fairly pedestrian from a musical point of view'. Szymczyk disagreed, maintaining that its power rivalled that of the title track. But lyrically, the main writer had done everything he set out to do. He was particularly proud of the last verse, which 'turns it from one thing into another and it becomes an allegorical statement about religion – the deception and destructiveness that is inherent in the mythology of most organised religion – the whole dominion thing'. Taken as a whole, he considered the song to be a reaffirmation of the time-honoured idea that everything in the universe was connected, with consequences for everything that mankind did.

Some years later, he commented that it remained one of his favourite songs as he cared more about the environment than about writing songs on drugs, love affairs or any other kind of 'excesses'. The message he meant to convey was that when mankind finds something good, he destroys it through his presence. He is the only animal on earth that is capable of wrecking the environment. It is still just as relevant, if not more so, than when it was first released.

The musical arrangement matches the power of the message. As a tune, it is relatively simple, proving that a songwriter can still compose a first-class melody with only three chords. A melancholy, softly tinkling piano intro sets the mood for the first verse, then equally subdued drumming appears on the second. Henley's vocals are deceptively relaxed at the start as he sings about how earlier generations unthinkingly laid the continent to waste. Organ, synthesiser and gentle steel guitar enter, building gradually yet subtly while the tone of the lyrics gradually becomes angrier as the stark finger-pointing narrative unfolds. After the fifth verse comes a seventy-second break as the synth, sounding like an orchestra, builds to a crescendo and negotiates a swift key change from E to G – then drums, synths cut out for a while as it returns to the tranquillity of the intro, a solo piano, then bringing the other instruments (including a few atmospheric seconds of ambient, seagull-like sounds) gently back in for the sixth.

The whole opus reaches a climax just before the start of the eighth and final verse, as synths sound like a celestial choir before Henley gives it everything he can, his voice taking some liberties with the melody as he hits the high notes in sheer passion, on the lines, 'And you can see them there on Sunday morning, stand up and sing about what it's like up there.' Close your eyes and you can almost imagine him clenching his fists as he sings, reaching new heights on the final 'goodbye' as his voice soars upwards.

After that climactic last verse, the same ascending five-note pattern slowly repeats itself in the coda for about a minute until the fade. Unlike most of their other songs, it doesn't mention the title in the lyrics, barely repeats a single line (apart from 'They called it paradise', a phrase that is central to the song's *raison d'être*) – and has no chorus. Moreover, it has a very cavalier approach to rhyming throughout. But such is the intensity of the band's performance, vocal and instrumental, and the power of the lyrics, that it matters not in the slightest.

It might have been tempting providence to consider releasing two epic singles from one massive seller of an album. But had the band not been spoilt for choice, resulting in 'The Last Resort' being relegated to B-side status for 'Life in the Fast Lane', it could have been another major hit for them. Bearing in mind the favourable critical reaction to it on release, the British arm of Warner Bros. may have missed another success by not flipping it over and promoting it as the A-side when it was apparent that 'Fast Lane' was not going to chart. As a lyricist and vocalist, Henley probably never quite reached the same remarkable standard again.

In Britain, Radio 1 presenter John Peel, who had recently reinvented himself as the BBC's champion of punk rock, openly subscribed to the new view that Eagles were bland and irredeemably uncool. Nevertheless, he was not immune to the song's spell, and admitted that notwithstanding what he thought of their image, he found 'The Last Resort' a powerful, moving piece of work, and played it regularly on his evening show during the summer of 1977. Some years later, music critic Dave Thompson called 'The Last Resort' 'even more weary and depressing' than Mitchell's 'Big Yellow Taxi', which masked a serious message in a chirpy singalong style complete with a spontaneous if inappropriate giggle in the last line. In allmusicguide.com, William Ruhlmann calls it 'a broad, pessimistic history of America that borders on nihilism'.

Hotel California was nominated for several Grammy Awards, including Record of the Year, which it won in March 1978, and topped the American album chart for six (non-consecutive) weeks. In commercial and artistic terms, it was going to be a hard, if not impossible, record to follow.

Exit Meisner, enter Schmit

Meisner had reached the end of the road. Feeling increasingly isolated, his physical and mental health suffering under the pressures and also substance abuse, he got into a couple of fights with Frey. At one point, shortly before the album was completed, Meisner, Felder and Walsh got together, decided they could no longer work properly with the other two, actively discussed breaking away once they had fulfilled their commitments, and forming a separate trio. A little later, two of them thought better of it, but Meisner was determined to leave, with or without them. Felder, who called him 'the sweetest man in the music business', and Walsh both begged him to stay, but he had had enough and walked out after the last date of the Hotel California tour in September 1977. Azoff's office issued a press release confirming that he had left, citing exhaustion as the reason.

As was the case after Leadon's departure had left a vacuum, there was one obvious replacement. Timothy B. Schmit, an easy-going, softly spoken character who played bass guitar and, as a vocalist, could reach the high notes with ease, had replaced Meisner in Poco in 1971. Six years later, he stepped into his shoes for a second time.

Standalone single
'Please Come Home for Christmas' (Charles Brown, Gene Redd) 2.57
'Funky New Year' (Henley/Frey) 3.59
Released November 1978 (US), December 1978 (UK)
The band had played 59 dates worldwide in 1977 and allowed themselves a less rigorous schedule the following year, with only 12 in America and five in Canada. In September 1978, shortly after they had started on the next album, initially planned as a double, Asylum asked them for something to fill the gap. For the first time, they agreed to record a standalone single. Szymczyk suggested something festive, and Henley, going back to his teenage days as an avid devotee of pop radio stations in Texas, immediately thought of 'Please Come Home for Christmas', co-written and first recorded by Charles Brown in 1960 and a minor Top 100 hit a year later. As it was a sweltering few days in Miami, when they gathered at Bayshore Studios, Coconut Grove, Florida, to record it, it took a leap of imagination for them to get into festive mode – 'perfect for a Christmas record' as Frey later quipped. Needs must where the devil drives. It was something British glamsters Slade had had to do at the Record Plant in New York to record their perennial 'Merry Xmas Everybody' during a brief break in an American tour, five hot summers earlier.

Eagles' version of the song stays closely to the original, apart from a minor lyrical change, singing 'bells will be ringing the sad sad news' at the start instead of 'glad, glad news'. Released in November, it charted at number 18, becoming the first seasonal single to reach the American Top 20 since Roy Orbison's 'Pretty Paper' in 1963, and re-entered the Top 50 at Christmas 2020.

In Britain, it made 30 in 1978. Another version, recorded by Jon Bon Jovi in Eagles style, that first appeared on the various artists charity album *A Very Special Christmas 2* in 1992, was extracted as a single two years later, credited to Bon Jovi (the band), and made the British Top 10. Eagles re-recorded it live in concert on New Year's Eve 1999, and it appeared on the 4-CD box set *Selected Works: 1972–1999* the following year.

The B-side of the 1978 single, 'Funky New Year' had B-side filler fodder written all over it. About 30 seconds of party noises with 'Auld Lang Syne' from a not-very-good lone sax player fades into a song with Henley on vocals again. He sings rather hoarsely about waking up on New Year's Day with a severe hangover after a riotous celebration the night before, and ad-libs towards the end 'whose shoes are these?' and 'what year is this anyway?' Musically, it was a workout that sounded like a cheerfully slapdash cross between The Average White Band and Stevie Wonder's 'Superstition' – apart from the fact that it never strayed from one chord throughout, with electric keyboards and guitar over a disco drum beat. Despite their apparent endorsement of The Bee Gees and a four-to-the-floor touch on 'One of These Nights' three years earlier, more recently, the band had made clear their disdain for the new music. Maybe they felt more threatened than they cared to admit by its domination of the singles and album charts for much of 1978, with the *Saturday Night Fever* soundtrack album maintaining a stranglehold on the top of the album charts for several months on end that year, on both sides of the Atlantic, and a host of other dance acts hot on their heels. As throwaways go, it's likeable enough.

Appropriately, the photo on the picture sleeve of the 1978 release (their first 45 to be issued thus in America and Britain) showed them in bathing trunks and sunglasses, relaxing on the patio of a swimming pool in midsummer, with a small fake white Christmas tree nearby.

Right: The first line-up of Eagles, 1973. Clockwise from bottom: Don Henley, Glenn Frey, Bernie Leadon, Randy Meisner.

Below: Eagles onstage at the Grand Ole Opry, Nashville, 2017. Left to right: Timothy B. Schmit, Vince Gill, Don Henley, Deacon Frey, Joe Walsh.

'Take it Easy', the debut single.

Left: a rare cover for promotional copies of the British issue.

Below: A Cashbox press ad for the American issue. (*Asylum*)

TAKE IT EASY *

Produced by GLYN JOHNS
*A single from EAGLES forthcoming album on ASYLUM RECORDS AS-11005

Right: The front of the first album, originally planned as part of a four-panel fold-out poster design until record company boss David Geffen thought it 'would be confusing'. (*Asylum*)

Left: The second album, a concept work based around the story of the Doolin-Daltons, a Wild West gang. (*Asylum*)

Right: Eagles, 1973, at around the time *Desperado* was recorded.

Above: Eagles, 1973, the year they began recording the third album, *On the Border.*

Below: Eagles, 1974, shortly after recruiting additional guitarist and 'late arrival' Don Felder (centre).

Right: The third album, recorded partly in England and partly in America, with a different producer for each. (*Asylum*)

Left: A British press advertisement for 'Already Gone', 1974, an American Top 40 success and UK turntable hit. (*Asylum*)

Right: Eagles, 1976, shortly after Leadon was replaced by Joe Walsh (second from right).

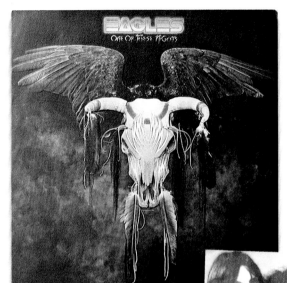

Left: The breakthrough fourth album, an American number one with a chart-topping single in the title track, and a British top ten record as well. (*Asylum*)

Right: The Belgian single of the title track, their first major international hit. (*Asylum*)

Left: The sheet music of 'Lyin' Eyes', a song dubbed by some of the band's former girlfriends 'Lyin' Guys'.

Right: The classic album that would later be certified America's third best-selling popular music long player of all time. (*Asylum*)

Left: The sheet music to the title track.

Right: Felder, whose reggae-style instrumental formed the basis for part of the title track, on stage in 1977. (*Asylum*)

PRODUCED AND ENGINEERED BY BILL SZYMCZYK FOR PANDORA PRODUCTIONS LTD

Left: The band's only standalone single, an early 1960s hit by Charles Brown, released appropriately on white vinyl in France. (*Asylum*)

Above: Bob Seger, co-writer of 'Heartache Tonight', onstage with new bass guitarist Timothy B. Schmit and Felder.

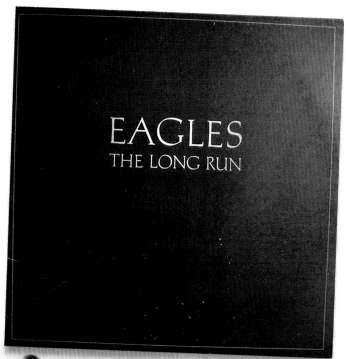

Right: The final album before the band dispersed, which Felder called their least favourite 'because it represented such a dark time personally'. (*Asylum*)

Left: Eagles, 1979: in their own words, 'sick and tired of each other'.

Left: The double live album, 1980, on which they fixed 'three-part harmony [vocals] and instruments courtesy of Federal Express'. (*Asylum*)

Right: Touring again in the new millennium, now as a quartet with additional players.

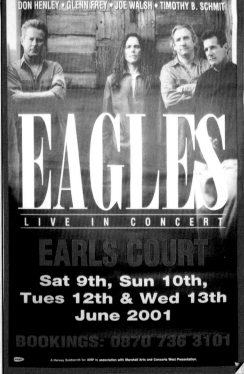

Right: Hell froze over and the famous five were back – for a few years. (*Geffen*)

Left: As Frey said on stage, 'For the record, we never broke up – we just took a 14-year vacation'.

Right: In 2001, 'Mr Felder' was fired, and then they were four again.

Left: The first all-studio album for 28 years, their sixth number one in the US and their first in the UK. It was Frey's swansong. (*ERC*)

EAGLES
HOW LONG

TAKEN FROM THEIR FIRST STUDIO ALBUM IN 28 YEARS

PROMOTIONAL USE ONLY : NOT FOR SALE

'LONG ROAD OUT OF EDEN' AVAILABLE OCT 30

Right: 'How Long', a one-track single issued on CD and 7" vinyl for promotional use only. (*ERC*)

Performing 'Hotel California' live on stage in Australia in 2010.

Right: Frey and Henley, the latter seen less often onstage behind his drums than in past years.

Left: Frey and Walsh, evidently sharing a joke.

Right: John David Souther and Jackson Browne in 2014. They were co-writers of several of the band's songs.

Left: Eagles leave the stage at Bossier City, LA, on 29 July 2015 – their final date with Glenn Frey.

Right: Henley on stage in 2019.

Left: A live album, recorded at The Forum, Inglewood, Los Angeles, over three nights in September 2018. (*Rhino*)

Right: Asylum so loved Bud Scoppa's review of the debut album that they used it in their press ads.

Left: A German 1977 reissue of two of the early songs, with Felder and Walsh on the sleeve though they played on neither.

Right: A Japanese picture sleeve of 'I Can't Tell You Why', the only A-side Schmit penned with the band.

Above: Eagles 2018, with newest members Vince Gill (second left) and Deacon Frey (centre).

Below: So ends another show in 2018.

The Long Run (1979)

Personnel:
Glenn Frey: vocals, guitars, keyboards
Don Henley: vocals, drums, percussion, synthesiser
Joe Walsh: vocals, guitars, keyboards
Don Felder: vocals, guitars, pedal steel guitar
Timothy B. Schmit: vocals, bass guitar
Additional personnel:
Jimmy Buffett, The Monstertones: backing vocals, 'Greeks Don't Want No Freaks'
David Sanborn: alto saxophone, 'The Sad Café'
Bob Seger: backing vocals, 'Heartache Tonight'
Joe Vitale: piano, electric piano, ARP string synthesiser
Produced by Bill Szymczyk and Eagles
Recorded at Criteria Studios, Miami; Record Plant Studios, Los Angeles
Record label: Asylum
Release date: September 1979
Highest chart positions: 4 (UK); 1 (US)
Running time: 42:50

To get a standalone single out of their star attraction a year earlier had proved moderately easy, but expecting them to deliver a new ten-track album in time for the Christmas rush was another thing entirely. Even the lure of a million dollars cash bonus failed to motivate them. And attempting to follow up such a groundbreaking, artistically and commercially successful album as *Hotel California* was going to be a thankless task. Eagles had returned to the studio in March 1978 for what they had initially planned as a double album. Frey said the decision had been taken thus, 'so that way no one worries 'is this the only song I'm going to get to do?'' Everyone would therefore get a chance to make what they felt was a fair contribution.

Yet it surely said something about Henley and Frey's joint lack of inspiration when the first track to be completed was a new song written largely as well as sung by their latest recruit. Ominously, the once-close partnership between both was breaking down. Arguments about trivial matters led to frayed tempers that almost ended up in fistfights. Both were involved in new relationships with women that were seemingly not going well. They agreed that they hated disco and the other new music, and after seeing negative press articles commenting that they had had their day, worried about whether they were still relevant or not. At least they were also of the same mind as regards environmental issues and opposition to the building of nuclear power plants. Eager to play benefit gigs for the right causes, they felt they were growing up and were tired of writing 'silly little love songs' now that more important things were happening.

Frey summed it up in an interview with Lloyd Bradley of *The Independent* in 1992. They had found out that lyrics were 'not a replenishable source', and had said a great deal on *Hotel California*. The problem they faced after that was 'what do we talk about now?' As members of Eagles, having spent much of the last few years creating music, rehearsing, recording and then playing it on tour across the world, 'we had far fewer real-life experiences to draw on.' Relationships between members had hit a new low, and Felder noted in his memoirs that it was their least favourite album 'because it represented such a dark time personally'. There was too much alcohol and drug abuse, too many egos, and worst of all, it had finally divided them into two camps, with the now-sparring Henley and Frey in one corner, and Felder himself with Walsh, the guitarists, in the other. Meanwhile, Schmit, 'the Wanderer', was probably wondering what on earth he'd let himself in for, and whether he'd joined a phenomenally successful outfit just in time to witness its death throes.

Henley realised they were physically, emotionally, spiritually and creatively exhausted, and badly missed living normal lives. He told *Rolling Stone* in 2016 that they needed time off and should have taken a break, 'but the big machine demanded to be fed'. Ironically it was a solution that Leadon had put to them four years earlier, and he had been spurned. But now they had peaked, they were keeping themselves going until they burned out, and now they had nothing more to say. If the company were more concerned with new product and more profits and had to have a new album, the suits would have to wait until he – or rather the band – were ready to resume work. Azoff thought, or took it for granted, that they would rediscover their creative spirit if they went out on tour again. They were still in demand as session players for the likes of Karla Bonoff, J.D. Souther and Bob Seger, and they contributed to another solo album by Walsh, *But Seriously, Folks...*, including his major hit 'Life's Been Good'. When Walsh joined Eagles, Henley had said the band was his first priority, and 'I don't think he cares if he ever makes another solo album'. It didn't take him long to prove Henley wrong. They also appeared on 'FM', a track by Steely Dan that was to be the title song to a forthcoming movie of which Azoff was executive producer. Moreover, as Frey said, if they were getting on each other's nerves, then was the time to move away for a while and work with others, a change being as good as a rest.

Sessions resumed in July 1978 but continued slowly, much to the consternation of Elektra-Asylum, who had been hoping for, if not expecting, a new album in time for Christmas. Desperate for any sort of product, the accountants pleaded for something, even if just a single, hence the recording of 'Please Come Home For Christmas'. They were not enthusiastic but realised it was better than nothing.

Not until early 1979 did everything start to come together again. As the band began work on new material, they gradually but slowly slipped back into the old creative process once more. Felder had three other songs partly ready for them to work on in addition to the two for which he had been partly responsible and which were used. With Henley, he had begun to develop them. One, 'You're Really High, Aren't You?' was a song of which the guitarist was really proud, and one of which they started before the drummer lost interest and never followed through. When asked many years later by *Rolling Stone* about it, Henley said it was just another one of the many joke titles they came up with and never recalled it becoming an actual song. If it did, it was just an instrumental presumably put on the back burner to await a set of lyrics that would never materialise.

The double album that had been visualised at first was clearly not going to happen, so instead of the 18 songs they had planned, much to Felder's annoyance, another single album was decided upon. He had made a special effort to contribute more ideas and demos and felt he had been wasting his time. At last, by the beginning of September, studio work was completed on *The Long Run*, or as they and the impatient company executives called it, 'The Long One'.

With hindsight, Henley, who had previously been renowned as the most painstaking member of all, would acknowledge that they had spent far too long on making it, and the process had become laboured. 'All one need do was listen to early Stones records to realise that all this striving for perfection is totally unnecessary.' Szymczyk had said on several occasions that Henley and Frey were the major nitpickers, and at last, he could understand that his precision hadn't been strictly necessary after all. *The Long Run*, he admitted, 'wasn't a very good album at all' and it depressed him to listen to it. 'We didn't have a good time making it; we were sick and tired of each other.' In *NME*, Nick Kent, who three years earlier had admitted a little guardedly to enjoying *Hotel California*, being impressed by the 'thought and work [that had] gone into its meticulous crafting', cared little for its successor. He called it ...

... a shallow, half-baked collection of songs that either repeat old formulae quite brazenly or else, in an attempt to expand the band's work in the precincts of oddball humour, find themselves stuck with an intriguing conceit for a title that chief composers Henley and Frey quickly discover they can't extend into anything of any consequence.

If The Beatles followed *Sergeant Pepper* with their 'white album', Eagles followed *Hotel California* with their 'black one'. Art director John Kosh needed minimal imagination to design a cover featuring four short words, but that was all they wanted. It was a stark, even funereal image that suited the bleak lyrics, as did the austere black, white and grey label design and the picture of five unsmiling band members. At least the inner sleeve photo of Szymczyk (excluded from some subsequent CD reissues), pointing to a card in front of him saying 'Hi Mom', injected a faint note of levity into the otherwise cheerless aura.

'The Long Run' (Henley/Frey) 4.27

The title track owes something to and reflects both writers' passion for
vintage Stax music, and also to 'Turning Point', an R&B hit in 1975 by Tyrone
Davis. For Frey, it was more like a tribute to the Memphis sound, with slide
guitars playing the horn parts and Felder adding organ.

Lyrically, the song suggests facing 'the long run' in the face of pressure,
and no matter what, 'we can go the distance – handle some resistance'. The
opening lines sing of the dilemma of someone who used to hurry and worry
a lot, and stayed out until daybreak until he or she saw it was time to quit
such a lifestyle – or, following on from a track on the previous album, try and
get out of living in the fast lane. Henley, whose lead vocal it was, said that
even if they were living such a frantic lifestyle, they could always idealise
about the way they really wanted to be.

It might have been a veiled message to their critics, a message from Frey
to him, from him to Frey, or to a long-departed lover. On the other hand, it
could have been irony, writing a song about longevity 'imploding under the
pressure of trying to deliver a worthy follow-up to *Hotel California*, and yet
we were writing about longevity, posterity'. Part of it was a belief in their own
ability to stay the course. Riled by articles in the press that it was written in
part as a response to articles that said Eagles were passé as disco was then
dominant and punk was also replacing the jaded old school of rock, thus the
taunt 'Who is gonna make it, we'll find out in the long run'.

The album's second single, it reached number eight in America and number
66 in Britain.

'I Can't Tell You Why' (Henley/Frey/Schmit) 4.57

The album's first completed song was begun by newcomer Schmit, who, in
his words, was going through a fraught emotional time. 'I was young and
confused about how to make relationships function, and this song was a
vent for my melancholia.' Having chosen the title and begun writing it in
a burst of inspiration, writer's block hit him, so he put it aside and then
passed what he had done so far to Henley and Frey. All three between
them completed it in a few all-night sessions. They were keen that Schmit's
first song with them wasn't going to be a country rock song, the kind of
material he had been singing with Poco, and Frey told him he could sing
like Smokey Robinson. The result was another Eagles soul tune, or as
Henley called it, 'straight Al Green'. Others might equally have called it
'straight Barry Gibb' with its smooth high-pitched harmonies, backed by
airy Fender Rhodes piano and Hammond organ from Walsh and Frey, and
string synthesiser from Vitale, rounded off by Felder's relaxed guitar solo
that plays out over the last two minutes.

As it was being mixed, they had an impromptu listening party at the studio,
and as everyone listened, Henley turned to Schmit and told him, 'There's
your first hit.' The album's third single faded to lose the last 20 seconds of

the album version, it reached number eight in America but failed in Britain. Subsequent cover versions were released by Howard Hewett in 1990, Brownstone in 1995 and Diana Krall in 2015.

'In the City' (Joe Walsh/Barry De Vorzon) 3.44

Henley and Frey weren't alone in finding it difficult to come up with new material for the album. Walsh was evidently short of inspiration as well, hence this out-of-character number that sounds more like a cut from one of his solo albums. 'In the City' had begun as a collaboration between him and Barry De Vorzon, an old friend who had written several film soundtracks and TV themes. He invited Walsh to write a song for *The Warriors*, a movie based on the story of nine members of the Coney Island Warriors, who were part of a plot to invite every street gang into an army capable of ruling New York, but were subsequently framed for their leader's murder and had to go on the run from police and rival gangsters. Walsh and De Vorzon wrote the lyrics after reading the screenplay. They express the usual aspirations of people born and raised in a dead-end environment, gazing at the horizon beyond the neon lights, yearning for a better tomorrow.

Frey, Henley and Szymczyk particularly liked the song and felt it had not achieved enough recognition as just one song in a movie – or else realised that reusing it on the album would help them to meet the deadline as well as give Walsh a cut of the royalties. Whatever the reason, it's one of the better tracks on a less than outstanding album, thanks largely to Walsh's searing slide guitar solo. The original version had female backing vocals, which were replaced here by Eagles harmonies.

'The Disco Strangler' (Henley/Frey/Felder) 2.46

Eagles had previously given disco their best shot in the title track of *One of These Nights* while it was still relatively fresh and owed something to classic soul, admitting that they enjoyed the Memphis and Philadelphia sounds that between them helped create the dance music explosion of 1974 onwards. Then the genre became inescapable, more and more punters tired of it, the backlash started and 'Disco sucks!' became the battle cry. 'Funky New Year' had been anything but a respectful homage to the genre, and the intentionally unpleasant 'The Disco Strangler' took this one stage further. Here we have a pulsating, and thankfully quite short, rather misogynistic number about a young woman on the town, dressed to kill (OK, an unfortunate turn of phrase, but as they wrote the lyrics, they must have known what would follow) as she struts her stuff on the dance floor as conspicuously as possible beneath the mirror ball, revelling in being drooled at by all the men. Lurking in the shadows is the disco strangler, 'the fiddler in your darkest night' (and no, we assume that doesn't mean he plays the violin), a crazed individual ready to put his hands around her throat. Felder admitted as much, while Szymczyk allegedly commented it was indeed a case of 'watch out for the guy on the date – he might have a knife.'

A funky rhythm guitar with an intermittent bass riff and drums to match supply the accompaniment to Henley's vocal, with no variation in chords or pitch throughout. Superficially it might have come across or been intended as satire or irony, but the meaning seems to have been deeper and more sinister than that. It was arguably filler of the worst kind, and the best thing that can be said about it was that they kept it reasonably brief – or else that Asylum resisted the temptation to issue a 12" disco mix in red vinyl. All the same, it does have its defenders, notably a round-up years later of 'Ten Eagles deep cuts' in *Classic Rock*, which called *The Long Run* their 'most under-appreciated album and their darkest', with 'this ball of wired disco-rock its most disturbing moment: a tense, nervous headache of a song that finds Henley casting a jaundiced eye over the mindless hedonism of the new generation.'

'King of Hollywood' (Henley/Frey) 6.27

This song makes it two utterly charm-free zones in a row, but unlike the preceding cut, 'King of Hollywood' does have a redeeming feature in that it proved eerily prescient. It was allegedly Henley's 'don't get mad, get even' two-fingered salute to the movie industry in Hollywood, especially the producers after he had been promised a role in a western picture and subsequently passed over. In an interview years later, he said that it was based on an incident that happened to his girlfriend.

The character portrayed in the song is a seedy individual who'll promise to make young, hopeful wannabes stars, if they do what he says. How badly does this sweet young innocent want the part? Is she willing to sacrifice everything, not least her reputation, and 'be real nice'? Speculation in online forums suggests that the song might have been about Harvey Weinstein, who in 2020 was convicted of sexual offences going back over three decades. This is unlikely as he was only just starting his career in 1979, but even so, Henley and Frey were outlining a scenario in the lyrics that would unhappily become far too commonplace in the seedier aspects of the movie industry.

However, once again, as in the previous track, little attention was paid to musical creativity. For over six minutes, the entire melody of this laid-back song, with its soft shuffle of drums and rhythm guitar, sits atop two chords. There is a small amount of modulation in the guitar break about halfway through as the pitch ascends, only to drop down again for the rest of the song.

'Heartache Tonight' (Henley/Frey/Bob Seger/J.D. Souther) 4.27

Turn over to side two – as it was on the original vinyl release – and the stylus hits the track that not only became the album's first single but also the best four minutes or so of the whole record. Long-time almost-but-not-quite-Eagle Souther makes the first of his three appearances as a collaborator. Inspired by some Sam Cooke oldies (rhythm-wise, the shuffle beat of 'Twistin' the

Night Away' springs to mind), Frey and Souther started this song off, the former clapping his hands to the beat as they came up with ideas, and the latter joining in. Henley's musical and lyrical contribution seems to have been slender, while Seger, Frey's long-time hero from Detroit from way back when also played an important role, supplying the title phrase and a couple of lines. According to one of Frey's interviews, Seger was there in the room at the time, coming up with ideas; in another, he said that he rang Seger on the phone to play him what they had already written, down the line. The former theory seems a little more likely. Although uncredited on vinyl and CD releases, Seger also contributed backing vocals on the chorus. He was repaying a compliment, as both Frey and Felder had played guitar on one track each of Seger's previous album, *Stranger in Town*, the previous year.

It's a bitter, if deceptively, catchy song. According to the first couple of lines, someone's going to come undone, or get hurt before the night is through. Despite that, Frey said that the song had 'no heavy lyrics', and it was intended to be 'more of a romp'. Yet it took on a more poignant air in 2016, when Seger played it at a memorial service for Frey, saying that 'he was always a positive force in my life.' Seger was sometimes asked to record the song himself or perform it live onstage, but he declined, saying it was at the highest end of his vocal range, and, therefore really difficult to sing.

This was Frey's only lead vocal on the album; Henley had five, and they shared two. On the recording, Walsh excels himself with some inimitable slide guitar work, while Henley lies down on the studio floor, holding a marching band-style drum on his chest that he beat with a mallet to produce the required sound. The percussion and handclaps, courtesy of Henley's Pollard Syndrum, were thought to have been inspired by another hit on the Asylum label the previous year, Andrew Gold's 'Never Let Her Slip Away', and would anticipate the increasing use of drum machines on his forthcoming solo work. Over the years, cover versions would be recorded by Conway Twitty, with The Osmond Brothers on backing vocals, Tom Jones on one of his TV shows, and a big band version by Michael Bublé.

'Those Shoes' (Henley/Frey/Felder) 4.57

A song apparently all about footwear had its origins in the band's fascination with girls wearing Charles Jourdan designer shoes, that had recently become very fashionable. From this, Henley and Frey decided to write a lyric that turned the shoes into a metaphor for women standing on their own two feet, so to speak, and taking responsibility for their own lives and losses. Once they'd started wearing 'those shoes', they weren't going to be naïve or malleable. They would become proper independent women, in charge of their own destiny, not merely decoration, or 'an appendage to some guy' who would take advantage of them.

Henley and Frey decided it would fit well with a recording from another set of guitar demos that Felder had recorded and overdubbed on his own. This one had been inspired partly by his love of jazz, above all by Miles Davis, who 'could play just a few notes and get so much soul in', and partly by the voice box effects that Walsh had used so effectively on his guitar in 'Rocky Mountain Way'. His intention was to work a section into one of their songs on which they could both play talkboxes, 'that sounded like two trumpets playing the melody'. Frey was thrilled with the idea, saying that to the best of his knowledge, it was the only double talkbox solo in existence. They ended up playing the backing track live in the studio with duelling guitar voices and no overdubs, the lead vocal being the only thing dubbed on afterwards. As they did so, they also brought a smile to everyone's face when they clearly sang 'butt out, butt out' near the end, leading Henley to remark that 'most of the humour is so dry nobody will think it's funny.'

The stuttering, almost funky guitar and drum beat used earlier in the song would later become a hip-hop sample used by the Beastie Boys on 'High Plains Drifter', a track on *Paul's Boutique* in 1989, and others.

'Teenage Jail' (Henley/Frey/J.D. Souther) 3.44

Quality control was clearly lacking on what is, by general consensus surely the worst song Eagles had yet committed to vinyl. Lifeless, tuneless, this slab of grunge sounds more like a Black Sabbath 45 accidentally played at 33 r.p.m. If the lyrics are trying to make any comment about youth and society, they fall far short – 'Wait for the weekend to go off the deep end, and make everything disappear' being a stock example. The guitar intro suggests something interesting to come, but it's one of those pieces that just seems stuck resolutely in bottom gear from start to finish. At the end comes a guitar solo from Felder, who said it was a four-in-the-morning, coked-out session that he always remained embarrassed to have played at all.

Frey was largely responsible for the song, and Felder admitted it was 'by far his worst writing effort'. At least Henley, who shared the vocal, and Souther, who also contributed, can share some of the blame as well. Henley admitted about ten years later that their humour 'actually got very dark and very sick' while they were making the album, and that came out particularly in 'Teenage Jail' (where any humour is so dark that it's well nigh invisible), and the following track, which for all its faults does actually rock.

'Greeks Don't Want No Freaks' (Henley/Frey) 2.21

Towards the end of the album sessions, the band watched the new movie *Animal House* and decided they ought to make things a little more light-hearted by creating their own pastiche of 1960s Farfisa organ-driven garage rock in the style of Question Mark and The Mysterians' classic '96 Tears'. The Beatles' 'Birthday' might also have been an inspiration. The presumably ad-libbed lyrics are nonsense or just rock 'n' roll revelry – beer all over the dance floor, a band playing rhythm 'n' blues, and so on. As Schmit commented, for once, they didn't need to be precise. It's basically about being loose and capturing the sense of fun with a bit of a party atmosphere. Jimmy Buffett and the ad hoc gang, alias The Monstertones, shouted backing vocals, and a good time was had by all. Including the listeners, until within less than two minutes, everything except vocals, drums (and handclaps) suddenly fade, leaving them to fade as well a few seconds later.

The song seems to feature near the top when music websites draw up a list of 'worst-ever Eagles songs'. Maybe the humour does verge a little on the dark side, but it wasn't meant to be taken seriously unless anyone wants to call them out for such a title on tenuously argued grounds of xenophobia or discrimination against people with disabilities. Freak having not been an offensive word in the 1970s, in the same way as recently gunned down and deceased outlaws on the back cover of the *Desperado* sleeve, might have been too stomach-churning in another age, it was a matter of 'attitudes of the time'. And they hadn't rocked as hard as this since 'Out of Control', six years earlier.

Having said that, some tracks on the album were good, occasionally very good. One or two were downright lame. This one is almost great – until that horribly premature ending. We all know songs can outstay their welcome ('Teenage Jail' certainly did), but this one rushes out of the door as it gets into its stride. Just as everyone's expecting the mother and father of guitar or sax breaks (or both) to send everyone on the dance floor wild – or turn into a seething party epic along the lines of an American answer to 'Brown Sugar' or 'See My Baby Jive' – it disappears within a few seconds. Were they really in that much of a hurry to finish it? Talk about a missed opportunity.

'The Sad Café' (Henley/Frey/Walsh/J.D. Souther) 5.35

What they knew at the same time was going to be their valedictory studio album (well, for nearly three decades) closes on a nostalgic note, an elegy to two of their favourite meeting places. In it, they reminisce about younger days spent at the Troubadour, and Dan Tana's restaurant next door. Souther, who said the song was 'more than anything else about losing your innocence, our innocence', recalled that they were both places where the future stars used to scheme, dream and laugh 'more than seems possible'. They took the song's title from *The Ballad of the Sad Café*, a collection of short stories by Carson McCullers published in 1951. In the album credits, the song was respectfully dedicated to John Barrick, their road manager who had died in the early days of their career.

It was one of Frey's favourite songs on the album as he loved the nostalgia it evoked of good and also bittersweet times. The line that resonated with him above all was, 'I don't know why fortune smiles on some and lets the rest go free.' It was a tale of looking misty-eyed at the Los Angeles scene when it had been buzzing with an air of optimism, young musicians on their way to a bright future, anything seemed possible for the taking. People had been warmer, more trusting, open and more forthcoming than they were now in the late 1970s, aged and embittered by their experiences and an often bruising brush with fame. By then, some friends and acquaintances of theirs from those early days had gone before their time, cases of 'too much, too soon' or 'too little, too late'. Was fortune a good thing or a bad thing, Frey asked, being fortunate before they were ready to deal with it, or were they struggling with their own success, riddled with feelings of guilt and unworthiness?

Lyrically it's the most thoughtful song of all, a slow, gentle number with Henley on vocal, but as a performance, it becomes rather bland, easy-listening fare if pleasant enough, verging uncomfortably close to the 'smarmy cocktail music' category that they had pooh-poohed only four years and two albums earlier. It includes a subdued but very distinctive guitar solo by Felder, inspired by a passage on Maria Muldaur's 'Midnight at the Oasis', and of which he remained proud. For the first time on an Eagles record, there is a saxophone break by jazz virtuoso David Sanborn – whose skills might have been better utilised on the previous track.

The album topped the American album charts for the last nine weeks of 1979, in statistical terms, a more impressive feat than they had managed in 1977 (when *Hotel California* had had to yield the coveted peak position to the massive sales of Fleetwood Mac's *Rumours* for week after week) and certified 26 million sales (26 x platinum). In Britain, it attained only gold status, a sharp fall after *One of These Nights* (platinum) and *Hotel California* (6 x platinum).

Eagles Live (1980)

Personnel:
Glenn Frey: vocals, rhythm guitar, keyboards
Don Henley: vocals, drums, percussion
Joe Walsh: vocals, guitars, keyboards
Don Felder: vocals, guitars
Randy Meisner: vocals, bass guitar (1976 dates)
Timothy B. Schmit: vocals, bass guitar (1980 dates)
Additional musicians:
Jage Jackson: rhythm guitar, percussion
Phil Kenzie: alto saxophone ('The Long Run')
Vince Melamed: electric piano ('New Kid in Town')
The Monstertones: backing vocals ('All Night Long')
J.D. Souther: vocals, acoustic guitar ('New Kid in Town')
Joe Vitale: piano, organ, drums, percussion
Produced and engineered by Bill Szymczyk
Mixed at Bayshore Studios, Florida
Mastered at Sterling Sound, New York City
Record label: Asylum
Release date: November 1980
Highest chart positions: 24 (UK); 6 (US)
Running time: 77:10
Tracklisting: 'Hotel California'; 'Heartache Tonight'; 'I Can't Tell You Why'; 'The Long Run'; 'New Kid in Town'*; 'Life's Been Good' (Walsh); 'Seven Bridges Road' (Steve Young); 'Wasted Time'*; 'Take It to the Limit'*; 'Doolin-Dalton'*; 'Desperado'*; 'Saturday Night'; 'All Night Long' (Walsh); 'Life in the Fast Lane'; 'Take It Easy'
All recorded 27–31 July 1980, Civic Auditorium or Long Beach, Santa Monica, California, except *20–22 October 1976, The Forum, Inglewood, California

Eagles had made several recordings on the first dates of the Hotel California tour in October 1976, and on the last few nights of The Long Run tour in July 1980. Henley seemed to have had more than one change of heart at around this time. One moment he was saying that before the last studio album sessions had been completed, he knew it was going to be their last one, then he would later contradict himself. After what was presumably one particularly good show on the tour, he admitted that he was getting tired, felt like quitting one day and then felt he could go on forever the next. But he was sure he could sustain their present level for at least one or two further albums, at least a studio set and a live record. 'What I'd like to do is make a really great studio album, maybe even a double album, to go out on. I'd like to go out gracefully rather than wait until it starts going down.' It was, in part, a very prescient comment, for within a little less than 30 years, he was involved in helping them make a remarkably good double album that looked like being their swansong (and would be for Frey).

75

But Azoff had warned a journalist that the thing that kept them together was the music, and if it didn't continue to hold them, everything could disintegrate in a second. Being nothing if not professionals, every night they put on a faultless show and received excellent reviews everywhere they went, although some writers thought that the most energy was coming from Walsh, who was bringing them some much-needed stage presence and turning them into 'a rock 'n' roll machine with plenty of guts'. With one eye on the Pete Townshend guide to music theatrics, sometimes he would threaten in jest to startle his more reserved fellow band members by smashing his acoustic guitar.

But by the time the tour finished that summer, everyone could see that they had had enough of each other. As they still contractually owed Asylum one album, they realised that a collection of performances from both tours would spare them the drudgery of creating anything new – let alone the purgatory of having to work with each other anymore. Not even an offer of $2 million from Asylum could persuade them to return to the studio together and deliver two new songs, one of which would doubtless become a farewell single – if not both. The album therefore consisted of live performances of numbers from every studio album except *On the Border*, plus two that had originally been released by Joe Walsh as solo efforts, and a concert favourite of theirs making its first appearance on record.

'Life in the Fast Lane' was the one track they recorded on the last night of the final tour, at Long Beach, California, on 31 July 1980. ('Life in the Last Lane'?) A fund-raiser for Democratic Senator Alan Cranston, the show proved to be the tipping point for two of the band. Felder disliked the idea of their being involved in political campaigns, and when Cranston's wife visited them backstage to thank them, he replied without much enthusiasm, 'Nice to meet you – I guess.' Frey, who was already at breaking point with him, was furious at this response. Onstage that night, he counted down on mic the order of songs remaining before he took Felder backstage to beat him up. Felder had the foresight to escape as soon as possible afterwards, making a hasty retreat in his limo after the gig was over.

So was the band – for now. By the autumn, Frey was not on speaking terms with the others, so he and Henley worked on mixing the recordings separately in Los Angeles and Miami, respectively. According to Szymczyk, who was working with his assistant in Los Angeles with Frey while the rest of the band were in Miami, they were were 'fixing three-part harmony [vocals] and instruments courtesy of Federal Express', as tapes with overdubs were regularly sent to and fro between the warring factions. When it was released, the harmonies were so perfect that the press suggested the band must have recorded it in the studio and added all the audience responses and applause afterwards. *Rolling Stone*, a journal with which they had long had a love-hate relationship, called it probably the most overdubbed live album in history, such criticism being rather unwarranted in that the previous few years could throw up many an instance of big-name bands having buffed their in-concert tapes to a sheen before even daring to consider releasing them on record. Szymczyk insisted that some of the tracks had been patched up as was customary with live albums but assured them that 70 per cent of the record was indeed live.

Several additional players and singers also appeared on the record. Among them were Jage Jackson, who also played on albums by Joe Walsh and Joe Vitale, the latter being a former member of Buffalo Springfield and then the Stills-Young Band; John David Souther, long-time associate of the band; Phil Kenzie, a Liverpool-born sax player whose numerous other credits included sessions with Al Stewart, Rod Stewart, Roger Daltrey, Wishbone Ash, Randy Meisner and Poco; and Vince Melamed, songwriter and occasional keyboard player who also appeared with Bob Dylan and Dan Fogelberg, and later formed Run C&W with Bernie Leadon. The Monstertones were an ad hoc backing chorus of friends and associates, including at times (though not all necessarily on this album) Jack Tempchin, Jimmy Buffett, Irving Azoff and tennis champion-turned-occasional rock guitarist John McEnroe.

The album sleeve design shows a concert tour storage chest that was used for band equipment.

'Life's Been Good' (Walsh) 9.38

As Walsh had already had some chart success as a member of The James Gang, Barnstorm and as a soloist prior to joining Eagles late in 1976, it was hardly surprising that the only two non-Eagles songs on the live album should have been tracks from his own career. 'Life's Been Good' had been a number from his third and by far his most successful album, *But Seriously, Folks...*, peaking at number eight in the US and number 16 in the UK. The full nine-minute album version had been edited to half the length for the single release, reaching number 12 in America and number 14 in Britain.

As Eagles didn't release an album as a group for almost three years (the length of the hiatus between *Hotel California* and *The Long Run*) and only one Christmas single in 1978 to fill the gap between 'Life in the Fast Lane' and 'Heartache Tonight', this solo effort was the next best thing. A sardonic view of the pampered rock star high life from one who had been there, it was welcomed by the music press, who appreciated the fact that somebody was actually telling it like it was. Over an ersatz reggae groove with sparring guitar and synths, Walsh's lyrics poke fun at himself, as he sings in the opening lines about having a mansion though he's forgotten the price – he's never set foot in it, but 'they tell me it's nice'. He's living in hotels, and if necessary, he'll hire two adjoining rooms and rip out the connecting wall – like that other noted rock 'n' roll hellraiser across the Atlantic, Keith Moon, he has accountants who will pay for any damage incurred. Fans write him letters, tell him he's great; his car does 185, but he's lost his licence, so he doesn't drive; he goes to parties until four, and it's hard to leave when he can't find the door. It's so tough, handling all this fortune and fame, but 'life's been good to me so far.'

It came as little surprise to the media, for Walsh had already had a name as the lovable clown who enjoyed sending himself and everyone else up, and was welcomed as being the one to put a little humour into what was widely seen as an over-earnest band. *Rolling Stone* called it 'the most important statement on rock stardom anyone has made in the late Seventies'. *New Musical Express* went one better in Roy Carr's reviews of the week's new singles in June 1978. He praised it as a record that ...

> ... hilariously demonstrates that G.I. Joe must be the only LA Megastar with both a perspective on the excesses of his profession and a droll Anglophile sense of humour. With good intent, Joe accurately lampoons himself and the overblown rockstar system into which he has been sucked by juxtaposing wry lyrics with sublime music. The skilled backing skips between Walshian power riffs and hokey reggae. Great as this record is, anymore of this nonsense and poor ol' Joe will be getting elbow from T'Eagles for blowing their cover. Must be on singles-of-the-year shortlist!

In 2013 Eminem used samples from it on *So Far...*, a track on *The Marshall Mathers LP 2*.

Frey, Henley and Schmit contributed backing vocals and Felder played guitar on other tracks on *But Seriously, Folks...*, but not this particular one. In spite of this, they come pretty close to reproducing the original full-length piece onstage, which at over nine minutes, is the longest track on the album. Vitale, a member of Walsh's band, was also on the line-up of the live album and probably plays drums. Walsh made a couple of minor alterations to the lyrics.

'Seven Bridges Road' (Steve Young) 3.54

Country music singer, songwriter and guitarist Young never achieved major success despite a long career that comprised over a dozen albums as a soloist. He had first recorded the song in 1969 on his debut album *Rock Salt & Nails*, which also included Gram Parsons and Gene Clark.

It is the only previously unreleased song on the live album, a showcase for their close harmony singing, as the verses of the song feature a cappella vocals from all five members. A single acoustic rhythm guitar is used from about 0.45 and finishes at 2.10. Their performance lasts about three minutes, the timing as given above, including almost a minute of applause and the announcement of the succeeding number.

They took their arrangement from a recording by Ian Matthews, formerly of Fairport Convention and Matthews' Southern Comfort, on his 1973 album *Valley Hi*, that Henley had bought at the time. At the time of its release, Matthews, Eagles and various other musicians were regulars at the

Troubadour, Santa Monica Boulevard, California, knew each other and often used to visit each other's houses to play and listen to music. For a long time Eagles would begin their stage show with the song. Having warmed up pre-concert by singing it unaccompanied together in a locker room shower area, they would perform it onstage, all singing into a single microphone. After releasing *Hotel California*, the album's title track replaced it as the opening number, although it had returned as the first item on the setlist by the time of the last tour. Felder said that it was for them 'always a vocally unifying moment, all five voices coming together in harmony', and it completely blew the audience away. Frey said they had modified their arrangement from hearing the original version, in 'a style that comes very easy and naturally to us'.

Matthews had recorded the song with producer Michael Nesmith (of Monkees fame), singing six- or seven-part harmony between them. Nesmith remarked with resignation that Eagles had lifted their arrangement note for note, but if 'they've got to steal it from somebody else, better they should steal it from me, I guess'. Young gave their version an equivocal welcome, saying he didn't like it at first because he thought it 'too bluegrassy, too gospel', but later admitted that he was warming to it the more he heard it.

It was issued as a single in America in December 1980, a month after the album, reaching number 21 in February 1981. Several European countries, excluding Britain, followed suit, in most cases with a different B-side.

'All Night Long' (Walsh) 5.40

The guitarist released this as a solo single in 1980; it appeared in the western movie *Urban Cowboy* that same year and reached number 19 on the American chart, although it never charted in Britain. This and 'Life's Been Good' remained the only American Top 20 singles of his entire career. The live version is almost two minutes longer. As a song, it's an engaging, catchy enough if a rather repetitive boogie shuffle.

This was the first live Eagles album to be officially released. The earliest in-concert recording to go on sale, excluding bootlegs, *Live at the Forum '76*, was first issued as the second disc in a three-CD 40th-anniversary edition of *Hotel California* in 2017. The ten tracks with a playing time of 48 minutes, taken from shows recorded from 20–22 October 1976 at the Los Angeles Forum, amounted to basically a 'Greatest Hits Live So Far' set, plus an early outing for the as yet unreleased 'New Kid in Town' and 'Hotel California', and Walsh's 'Funk #49'. It is chiefly notable for a guest appearance by J.D. Souther on acoustic guitar and backing vocals on 'New Kid In Town'. At the time of writing, its only issue as a standalone package has been as a double LP on black vinyl, with three playing sides and a fourth etched with an image from the front sleeve design, a graphic based on the original *Hotel California* cover. According to Peter Watts in *Uncut*, it's probably their best live album, with the band 'playing their home territory at pretty much the height of their powers', as well as presenting most of their best work to date 'in an easily digestible form with almost no filler.'

From Long Run to long break

To all outward appearances, after the last date of the tour, Eagles ceased to exist without making any official announcement that they had split. Not long after that miserable evening at Long Beach, Frey rang Henley to tell him he planned to begin work on a solo project. Henley said afterwards that he was 'shocked and hurt', but with a sense of horrible relief, he recognised that the band was finished. It had dawned on him after they had recorded *Hotel California* that he and Frey were growing in opposite directions, as he wanted to write more about social issues and Frey didn't. The record company and management, he went on, did nothing as they were sure they would change their minds. But all band members 'were in a dark place', doing too many drugs and under too much pressure. They should have taken a year off or hired a psychiatrist.

In January 1981, *Live* was certified platinum for one million sales, and at the eighth annual American Music Awards, they won the Favourite Band and Favourite Album categories. In May 1982, Azoff came clean and belatedly announced what everyone more or less knew – that they had gone their separate ways. Frey told the press that they had realised halfway through recording *The Long Run* that he knew it would be their last studio album. He started the band, he got tired of it and so he quit. When questioned about getting back together, he said that he completely ruled out 'the possibility of putting Eagles back together for a Lost Youth and Greed tour'. Henley vowed tersely that they would reunite 'when hell freezes over'.

In November 1982, Asylum issued a *Greatest Hits Volume 2*. Eight of the ten tracks were taken from the last two studio albums, plus 'Seven Bridges Road' (live), and 'After the Thrill is Gone', an apt comment on where they were at (or weren't) at the time. Any hopes of it being a worthy successor in sales terms to the first compilation were dashed when it peaked at a modest 52 in America and failed to chart in Britain, though in two of their most loyal markets, Australia and New Zealand, it reached number five and number two respectively. The band were annoyed by its appearance, Henley dismissing it as 'a big rip-off'. The best thing that can be said in its favour is that every member from the 1971–80 line-ups appears on at least one track.

By now, the solo projects had started coming. Not surprisingly, those by the two frontmen would be the most successful by a mile. During the 1980s, Henley's three albums, *I Can't Stand Still* (US and UK 24), *Building the Perfect Beast* (US 13, UK 14), and *The End of the Innocence* (US 8, UK 17), all charted strongly, spawning four American Top ten singles between them. From the second album, 'The Boys of Summer' was an American top five single, reaching number 12 in Britain in 1985 and repeating the feat on reissue in 1998. It was also covered in widely differing styles three times in the 2000s, with a dance version by DJ Sammy reaching number two in Britain and a more punky one by The Ataris making the Top 40, both in 2003, followed by easily the best of all, a folk-rock retread by The Hooters on their album *Time*

Stand Still in 2007. Henley also recorded a duet with Patti Smyth, 'Sometimes Love Just Ain't Enough', a number two American and top 30 hit in Britain in 1992. By around this time, he was suffering from a bad back, the legacy of too many years of drumming and singing simultaneously. He would now be seen onstage more often than not playing either rhythm guitar as he sang, a more appropriate instrument for a soloist or frontman who was now the undisputed leader of his band, or else standing centre stage at the mic with no instrument at all.

Frey enjoyed three American Top 40 albums, *No Fun Aloud*, *The Allnighter*, and *Soul Searchin'*. A single from the second, 'The Heat Is On', featured in the film *Beverly Hills Cop*, giving him a number two American and number 12 British hit in 1985. As his records became less successful, he tried his hand at acting on TV, a sideline that came to an end after he appeared in a drama series *South of Sunset* as a private eye. It was cancelled after the pilot episode was panned by critics and attracted poor viewing figures.

All the other ex-members released material, mostly as solo artists, during the decade but with little success. Walsh continued to release solo projects throughout the 1980s, the most successful being *There Goes the Neighborhood* (1981) reached number 20 and *You Bought It – You Name It* (1983) number 48. He retained a high profile on the session scene, contributing guitar to albums by The Beach Boys, Steve Winwood, John Entwistle and Michael McDonald. From 1989 onwards, he was a regular touring member of Ringo Starr's All-Starr Band (keeping it in the family, Mrs Walsh and Mrs Starr being sisters), and Schmit also played with the former Beatle on a couple of tours in the 1990s.

Two albums by Meisner reached the Top 100, the first, *One More Song*, spawning two Top 30 hits – 'Deep Inside My Heart', a duet with Kim Carnes, number 22 and 'Hearts on Fire' number 19. He also toured with his own band, The Silverados, but was happier leading a quiet life at home than appearing on the concert stage.

Schmit recorded two albums on his own, *Playin' it Cool* (1984) and *Timothy B.* (1987). Neither made the top 100, although a single from the second, 'Boys' Night Out', reached the top 30. He also toured as a backing vocalist with Toto in 1982 and Jimmy Buffett a year later, as well as playing and singing on sessions for Henley, Bob Seger and Boz Scaggs.

Felder's solo career began promisingly in 1981 with the single 'Heavy Metal (Takin' a Ride)', the theme song to the animated cartoon *Heavy Metal*. Recorded with Henley and Schmit, it reached number 43. He was also in demand as a session guitarist at this time, playing on albums by The Bee Gees, Andy Gibb, Diana Ross and Barbra Streisand. A solo album, *Airborne*, which featured Schmit, Kenny Loggins and former Traffic guitarist Dave Mason on backing vocals, followed in 1983. It spawned a minor hit in 'Never Surrender', co-written with Loggins, which appeared on the soundtrack of the movie *Fast Times at Ridgemount High*. Henley invited Felder to go on tour with him in 1985, but he turned it down, preferring to spend more time at home with his wife and children, and working with others in the studio. Leadon was the least active as a recording artist. With The Bernie Leadon-Michael Georgiades Band he made an album *Natural Progressions* (1977). Eight years later, he was part of Ever Call Ready, a bluegrass and gospel band, with ex-Byrds guitarist and mandolin player Chris Hillman, Al Perkins and fiddler David Mansfield, and they recorded an album under the same title. For a while, he also played with The Nitty Gritty Dirt Band and Run C&W, a novelty band playing Motown oldies in bluegrass style. He finally recorded and released a solo album under his own name, *Mirror*, in 2004, produced by Glyn Johns' son Ethan, who also played several of the instruments.

Most of these solo albums were good enough to merit a critical rating of at least three stars out of five, and the singles by Schmit and Felder fitted well into the contemporary 1980s soft rock genre. With more exposure, some of these would surely have charted. But Henley and Frey remained the undisputed masters, and the media showed little interest in the others.

The almost simultaneous success of Henley and Frey in mid-1980s Britain led to both promoting their current hits as they mimed or sang to a backing track with their own bands on BBC TV's weekly *Top of the Pops*, a British institution on which they never appeared during Eagles' lifetime despite five Top 30 UK singles in the previous decade. It also resulted in another compilation, *The Best of Eagles*, that reached number eight and was rarely out of the Top 100 British album chart for nearly a decade, although not issued in North America.

Yet speculation continued as to if and when the band would make up and be friendly. At the end of September 1989, Henley and Frey were seen onstage together for the first time in over nine years. During two of the final dates of Henley's American tour at the Universal Amphitheatre in Los Angeles and at the Pacific Amphitheatre in Costa Mesa, during the last show in Costa Mesa, he said that people were always asking whether they were going to reunite. He didn't know, 'but here's the next best thing – my good friend, Glenn Frey'. Putting down his guitar, he returned to the drums for 'Hotel California' and 'Life in the Fast Lane', while Frey played guitar and sang harmony vocals. Rumours soon gained currency and were fuelled further in April 1990 with a benefit festival for the Walden Woods Project, an environmental organisation dedicated to preserving the forest in Massachusetts that had been greatly loved by Henry David Thoreau, the 19th-century naturalist and poet. To protect the area from the ravages of property developers and the mining industry was a cause dear to Henley's heart. Never one to miss an opportunity, Irving Azoff suggested that Henley and Frey ought to get together and write a couple of new songs, with all profits going to the fund. To his astonishment, Henley said yes. After he had played a nine-song set of favourites from his 1980s albums to deafening cheers, he brought Frey and Schmit onstage to join him in an eight-song set of Eagles greatest hits.

But it was far from a done deal. In an interview with Lloyd Bradley in *The Independent* two years later, Frey was careful not to raise expectations. He said that he only had to mention he was interested in the idea of reforming Eagles, and two days later, he would be reading in the papers about a reunion and tour. He and Henley had already discussed doing so, but they 'could not get it together artistically or personally', and felt they had simply drifted too far apart.

They had reckoned without Azoff's persistence. On a few occasions, he rang Felder up to say he was hoping to 'get the guys together in the same room sometime', but the guitarist became frustrated with nothing further happening. He contacted Schmit and Walsh, who were both interested in putting together a partial Eagles. For a vocalist, Walsh recommended Terry Reid, an English singer whose track record had included coming close to joining Led Zeppelin until he had suggested Robert Plant would be better. Unfortunately, Reid had an alcohol problem, while Walsh was grappling with a drug habit as well, and in no fit state to join another band. Felder and Schmit accordingly recruited another English singer, Paul Carrack, at various times keyboard player and sometimes also vocalist with Ace, Mike and the Mechanics, Roxy Music and Squeeze, and Max Carl, formerly of .38 Special. They recorded a few tracks at Felder's home studio in Malibu, including a song written by Carrack with British songwriter Peter Vale and former Traffic drummer Jim Capaldi, 'Love Will Keep Us Alive'. Azoff's initial reaction was so enthusiastic that they thought a deal would be forthcoming. While in the process of toying with a suitable name, such as Big Sky, Big Party, or even in desperation (and not very seriously) Malibu Men's Choir, a few days later, Azoff faxed a furious Felder to say that the material they had submitted wasn't up to standard.

In November 1990, Azoff contacted all five members, and each of them responded positively. Henley, Felder and Schmit gathered at various studios and prepared to carry on where they had left off. Walsh kept them waiting and, after a few false starts, showed up, although evidently still 'under the influence'. Much to their amazement, once he plugged his guitar in he blew everyone away with a solo that proved he had lost none of his prowess. Meanwhile, Frey was sending them messages that he would soon show up, until one day when a clearly angry Azoff arrived to tell the ever-more impatient four that he had decided against it. They wondered whether he'd ever agreed in the first place, or whether Azoff had been leading them on in the hope that he might come.

They briefly toyed with the idea of continuing without him, but Henley shook his head and the others wearily agreed. It later emerged that Frey's no-show might have been partly related to surgery to remove part of a damaged intestine. Whatever his reasons, his subsequent threats to take legal action if they tried reforming Eagles without him meant the whole scheme was dead in the water.

But Azoff still knew when to seize any possible opportunity. A year or two later, he began persuading a handful of Nashville musicians, mostly from the younger, newer generation, to record an album of Eagles songs on his own newly formed label, Giant. Several of them, though no former Eagles themselves, had participated in another Walden Woods benefit concert in 1992 and told Henley how much the band's music had originally inspired them. The result was a tribute album, *Common Thread: The Songs of the Eagles*, with royalties going to benefit the Woods. Among the artists taking part were Vince Gill, Suzy Bogguss, Clint Black and Tanya Tucker, with Gill's version of 'I Can't Tell You Why' including Schmit on backing vocals.

None of the others took any part in the recordings, but Travis Tritt wanted to record a video for 'Take It Easy' and was keen for all five members to take part in the filming. When they agreed, the resulting video shot in December 1993 marked the first time they had all been seen together since that ill-tempered farewell gig in July 1980. The intense interest generated by the album, song and video led to what one record executive called 'Eaglemania'. A succession of carefully arranged phone calls and meetings, and positive responses from all five, resulted in what gradually became a fully-fledged reunion, or as Frey called it, 'a resumption'. As Felder soberly noted, it was amazing 'how a few zeros on the end of a check can make you forget how much you dislike someone and justify your putting up with them again after all these years'. Walsh was informed gently but firmly that he had to 'get clean', while Frey admitted that he had no idea how long it would all last. Schmit, who had joined the band just in time for what had looked like their final studio album, was delighted. He cited the Rolling Stones as a prime example of an outfit that had remained together, despite their joint driving forces often not seeing eye to eye. 'That's what it finally came down to. Let's do this thing and come together and work again.'

Despite the continuing uncertainty about how fully committed they all were to making it work, Azoff gleefully informed the media that 'Hell has frozen over.'

Hell Freezes Over (1994)

Personnel:
Glenn Frey: vocals, guitars, keyboards
Don Henley: vocals, drums, percussion, acoustic guitar
Joe Walsh: vocals, guitars, slide guitar, organ
Don Felder: vocals, guitars, pedal steel guitar, mandolin
Timothy B. Schmit: vocals, bass guitar
Additional personnel:
John Corey: piano
Scott Crago: percussion, drums
Timothy Drury: vocals, keyboards
Stan Lynch: percussion
Jay Oliver: organ, piano
Paulinho da Costa, Gary Grimm: percussion
Brian Matthews: electro-theremin
Al Garth: trumpet ('New York Minute')
Burbank Philharmonic Orchestra (7–11, 15)
Produced by Eagles, Elliot Scheiner, Rob Jacobs and Stan Lynch ('Learn To Be Still' only)
Live tracks recorded at Warner Burbank Studios; studio tracks at The Village Recorder and Sounds Interchange, Toronto, 25–26 April 1994
Record label: Eagles Recording Co./Geffen
Release date: November 1994
Highest chart positions: 18 (UK); 1 (US)
Running time: 72:36
Tracklisting: 1. 'Get Over it' (Henley/Frey); 2. 'Love Will Keep Us Alive' (Pete Vale/Jim Capaldi/Paul Carrack); 3. 'The Girl From Yesterday' (Frey/Jack Tempchin); 4. 'Learn To Be Still' (Henley/Stan Lynch); 5. 'Tequila Sunrise'; 6. 'Hotel California'; 7. 'Wasted Time'; 8. 'Pretty Maids All in a Row'; 9. 'I Can't Tell You Why'; 10. 'New York Minute'; 11. 'The Last Resort'; 12. 'Take It Easy'; 13. 'In the City'; 14. 'Life in the Fast Lane'; 15. 'Desperado'

After several weeks of rehearsals during the early weeks of 1994, the first live performance of the newly reformed (or 'resumed') band took place in April at the Warner Bros. studios in Burbank, California, for an MTV special. The show began with Frey telling the audience, 'For the record, we never broke up – we just took a 14-year vacation.' They then played a selection drawn from each of their previous albums apart from *On the Border*, plus a Don Henley solo track.

As was customary with their stage shows, most of the songs closely followed the original studio versions, with very little scope for improvisation or interpolation from quotes or riffs from other songs, whether their own or those of others. The most significant differences were on 'Hotel California', which was extended by a longer introduction from Felder on acoustic guitar, played twice – the first time solo, the second with a gentle tap on the drums. The moment that familiar chord sequence raised its head, the enthusiasm of the audience as they recognised it was evident. The final verse of the song was followed by a dual acoustic guitar break from Felder and Walsh, almost wandering into flamenco territory at times. 'Take It Easy' also enjoyed the minor makeover of an extended break on guitars (and no banjo in sight), resulting in its being extended by about a minute more than the original 1972 take, while 'In the City' finished with a slowed-down reprise of the guitar riff from the intro of The Beatles' 'Day Tripper'. Before they played 'The Last Resort', Henley said, 'Everyone's heard of how the West was won; well, this is about how the West was lost.' His words were left intact on the DVD but edited from the CD.

When he heard the results, Meisner was unimpressed with the new 'Hotel California'. What, he asked, was the point in their redoing the original, of tampering with such a classic recording, apart from making money? It was pretty, he said, but it just didn't sound the same. Where finance was concerned, he had a valid point. It angered him that as the old songs had been newly re-recorded, neither he nor Leadon would benefit from sales, airplay or performance royalties. The omission of 'Take It to the Limit' looked like a deliberate snub to exclude him, as the only way both of them would reap any advantage would be from a new surge in sales of the old albums.

One minor difference that would never be heard (intentionally) was on 'Desperado', a song that didn't require the input of all five members onstage. Since joining the band, Felder and Walsh had found their own way of keeping themselves entertained as they sat at the back, not miked up, looking as if they were singing harmonies – when in fact, they were mouthing something facetious like 'Desert rat hole', 'Avocado', or 'El Dorado', to keep boredom at bay.

Scott Crago, a session musician who had played drums on the two previous Bee Gees albums, was among the supplementary musicians on the record. He toured with them extensively thereafter, freeing Henley up to concentrate more on rhythm guitar and vocals.

'New York Minute' (Henley/Danny Kortchmar/Jai Winding)

The only song from the live set that had not originally been an Eagles song was a track from Henley's third solo album *The End of the Innocence*, released in 1989. Although it was one of his less successful singles, reaching number 48 in America and registering fleetingly in the British Top 100 for one week, it later became regarded as one of his finest moments. At the concert, he announced it as a song 'about appreciating what you have'.

It was partly inspired by the Wall Street crash of October 1987, with the mood of despair it created in the city, and the brief description in the opening lines of a suicide. (Followed, interestingly, by a quote from a Paul Anka song made famous by Buddy Holly, 'But I guess it doesn't matter anymore'.) Some years later, it took on a new significance in the aftermath of the events of

9/11. Its graphic description of the song's narrator walking home one autumn or even early winter evening through 'the groaning city in the gathering dark', is one of several atmospheric images painted in the lyrics. In a New York minute, he sings, everything can change; 'take care of your own, one day they're here, next day they're gone.' Despite its downbeat mood, it ends on a note of hope, with its assurance that 'I know there's somebody somewhere, make these dark clouds disappear.'

The lyrics were Henley's work, while the music was jointly written by Danny Kortchmar, a session guitarist and keyboard player who had worked extensively with such artists as James Taylor, Linda Ronstadt and Neil Young and others, as well as collaborating as a co-writer with Henley on much of his solo material. Session keyboard player Jai Winding likewise had worked with many other artists of the same genre, including Jackson Browne, Bonnie Raitt and Warren Zevon.

On this performance as well as the other five with strings, the 'Burbank Philharmonic' was an ensemble of studio-based classical musicians who had regularly played on movie soundtracks. While they were rehearsing the song for the show, Henley complained to the conductor that the orchestra were 'playing like trained people', but it was pointed out to him that as professional orchestral members, that was what they were. 'It's meant to be the blues, man,' he retorted. Fortunately, they were sufficiently well versed in varying their approach when necessary to accommodate the most demanding of rock performers.

New songs
'Get Over It' (Henley/Frey) 3.33

Henley, who sang lead, was very proud of this song, 'written in a burst, the fastest song, tempo-wise, that we've ever recorded'. It had got him and Frey in the same room together again after 14 years, and they created something together, 'even if it wasn't the best thing we ever wrote'. They had been less than confident about resuming the old partnership after such a long interval, and this showed them that they need not have worried.

Although Eliot's biography *To the Limit* speculates on its being more than anything else 'a comical, good-natured nod at the feud' between its two joint creators, Frey asserted that its inspiration came from elsewhere. He said it came from their intense dislike of tabloid television, stuffed to the gills with professional victims everywhere they looked, all over the media, and their being sick and tired of people moaning that whatever had happened to them was somebody else's fault. – 'All this whinin', cryin', pitchin' – get over it, get over it!' Henley offered him the title before they had come up with any lyrics, but most of the lines were his, with the occasional word or idea from Frey. Even Shakespeare is referenced in one verse, 'The more I think about it old Billy was right, let's kill all the lawyers, kill 'em tonight' being adapted from a line in The Bard's *Henry VI*, Part II, Act IV.

The spirit of the lyrics is anything but comical or good-natured. In the last verse, the closing line, 'I'd like to find your inner child and kick its little ass', provoked some criticism, especially from one online commentator on a forum that argued how the concept of the 'inner child' had aided his own recovery from a history of child abuse and alcoholism, and that nobody ever taught a child not to hit by hitting them. At the same time, others applauded its cocking a snook at excessive political correctness, making a stand against a society that had become too litigious for its own good, and the maxim that 'where there's blame, there's a claim'.

Of the four new songs, it certainly rocks the hardest, with a scorching guitar break that matches the intensity of the lyrics.

'Love Will Keep Us Alive' (Pete Vale/Jim Capaldi/Paul Carrack) 4.03

The one new song into which none of them had had any creative input was to become the most popular in terms of airplay. Schmit takes lead vocal on a ballad that was the sole remaining legacy from the sessions at Felder's house that had almost been the start of a new band, with Carrack originally singing lead. The result was a charming ballad that has something of a soul vibe and wouldn't have sounded out of place on a Bee Gees album. Released as a single in Britain, it gave them two weeks of singles chart glory with a peak of 52.

Although he felt vindicated to some extent that it had been recorded and released on album, Felder thought it spoke volumes that a track Azoff had scathingly rejected, perhaps in a mood of impatience, was now deemed worthy of inclusion. Carrack saw it a little differently: 'Everything was fine and dandy, when much to my chagrin, they came to their senses and put the Eagles back together. That was the end of my little project.' Yet it was the beginning of Eagles' second coming, and probably earned him far more royalties than an unsuccessful single and totally ignored album by an Eagles spin-off could ever have done.

'The Girl From Yesterday' (Frey/Jack Tempchin) 3.24

Frey's songwriting partnership with Tempchin had continued throughout his solo years, notably on 'Smuggler's Blues', the second and last of his British hits. His only lead vocal on the four new songs was one that had been intended for the next album he would record on his own, a break-up song about the end of an affair, the boy deciding that the girl is now part of his past. It was written from real life, about his ex-wife Janie, to whom he had been married from 1983 to 1988. According to Tempchin, he and Frey wrote it together shortly after the latter's divorce and remarriage. Once they had reached the last verse, were both characters going to get together again or not? No, they decided – she may be waiting by the phone for a tender word from him again, or at least the reassurance that he might be coming back, but she would remain 'the girl from yesterday'.

It's a pleasant enough, bittersweet country song, very close in style to much of their early material. The others in the band cared little for it, Felder scathingly commenting that if they hadn't allowed the record company to 'slip something mediocre onto the disc, they wouldn't have anything on the album at all' – and that was particularly true of this song, which had everybody's eyes rolling. When Frey was out of the studio, Henley admitted that it was not his best work and any country singer from Nashville could have sung it better. They added it to the setlist for their forthcoming tour, but it never went down well live and was soon dropped.

'Learn To Be Still' (Henley/Stan Lynch) 4.28

Mostly Henley's creation as well as his vocal, with a little input from Stan Lynch, former drummer with Tom Petty and the Heartbreakers, the last new song was a straightforward acoustic ballad. To Eliot, it was one of four quite ordinary songs that 'did nothing so much as underscore to the audience how powerful and lasting the band's classic body of work really was'. Others take the view that it's a simple but very effective, even charming number with the simple message in the title about taking time to relax, enjoy the more positive, peaceful aspects of the world around you, and be satisfied with what you've got. If the flowers in your garden don't smell so sweet, 'maybe you've forgotten heaven lying at your feet'. As their first great record said, 'don't let the sound of your own wheels drive you crazy'. Twenty-two years later, another song, inspired by the writer's studying of the works of Thoreau and others, says it differently. Lush acoustic guitars, subtle synths and drums, and unobtrusive lead guitar all help to create a mood that brings to mind some of George Harrison's more reflective works.

The Hell Freezes Over tour began on 27 May and was originally scheduled to comprise 70 shows across America until December. Relations between all five members did not remain harmonious for long, with reports of each member travelling in separate vehicles, and there was a four-month hiatus when Frey, who had suffered from diverticulitis for some time, needed to take time off for surgery and recuperation.

The album was released in November 1994 and entered the American album charts at number one, staying there for two weeks. A DVD was also released, featuring three additional tracks, 'Help Me Through The Night', a Walsh song that had previously appeared on his 1974 solo album 'So What', another Henley number from *The End of the Innocence*, 'The Heart of the Matter', and a remix of 'Seven Bridges Road', remastered from the 1980 live album. 'Get Over It' was released as an American single and reached number 31, while in Britain, 'Love Will Keep Us Alive' peaked at number 52.

After the final date of the tour at Murrayfield Stadium, Edinburgh, in August 1996, the band went on hiatus. About a year later, they called a band meeting, discussed new songs of their own, plus demos from other Nashville songwriters, and decided that in future, they would produce themselves. When they went into the studios, they tried out a handful of numbers, including 'I Love To Watch a Woman Dance', 'Downer Diner', and 'Little Latin Lover'. Despite a few months of sporadic attempts to make everything work, a combination of bickering between Frey and Henley and their complaining constantly about the other one when backs were turned, a general consensus that the songs simply weren't good enough, and a general lack of focus, resulted in Henley pulling the plug. Felder took a few tapes home to carry on working with, but as he feared, nobody else had the resolve to take it any further.

In January 1998, they were inducted into the Rock and Roll Hall of Fame in New York. It was preceded by arguments as to whether both former members, as well as the current five-piece line-up were entitled to be present. Fortunately, VH1, which was covering the presentation, made it clear that they wanted all seven playing together. To all outward appearances, it was a harmonious evening, but in private, the atmosphere was tense, mainly as Frey and Henley had not really wanted Leadon or Meisner there. Everyone took the stage after each had made their own individual address of thanks as planned, to play 'Take It Easy' and 'Hotel California', with Meisner miming on the left, and Leadon on the right barely playing at all.

The following year, contact resumed between the band members (but excluding the two ex-members) about recording some more new material and playing some end-of-the-millennium shows in December 1999, two in Las Vegas and one in Los Angeles. Azoff had decided that it would result in another live album for a box set that would give them time to record the next studio album. A plethora of compilations had been unleashed across the universe, among them a new 17-track *The Very Best of the Eagles,* in 1994 that spent over two years on the British album charts and peaked at number four, although again, it was not available in North America. The same collection was reissued in Britain in 2001 with similar packaging but the same tracks in a different, non-chronological sequence, with a high of number three during a 67-week run.

Selected Works, 1972–99 (2000)

The first Eagles compilation to offer more than an assortment of previously released material was a 53-track, four-CD collection released in November 2000 in a long-form box with a 44-page book. It only reached number 109 in America, but number 28 in Britain, number two in New Zealand and number eight in Australia. The first three discs ('The Early Days', 'The Ballads', 'The Fast Lane') comprised studio material, including three studio outtakes, and the fourth ('The Millennium Concert') comprised 12 tracks from their show at the Staples Center, Los Angeles, on 31 December 1999.

For Felder, who was suffering from a severe bout of influenza and on heavy medication, it would unknowingly be the last time he ever took the stage with the others. In February 2001, he was fired from the band, with Azoff telling him on the phone that Henley and Frey considered it was in the best interests of the band if they let him go. He filed two lawsuits against them, alleging wrongful determination and breach of contract, claiming that from 1994 onwards, both founder members had demanded and received a higher percentage of the band's profits, whereas such sums had previously been divided jointly between all five. They counter-sued Felder for breach of contract, alleging that he had written and attempted to sell the rights to a 'tell-all' book about his life with the band. The book *Heaven and Hell: My Life in the Eagles* was published in 2006, and one year later, the case was settled out of court for an undisclosed amount. The bitterness between both sides was never healed, and from then on, Henley and Frey always referred pointedly in interviews to their former guitarist as 'Mr Felder'.

Felder was replaced by Steuart Smith, who played guitar, mandolin and keyboards. A former member of Henley and Frey's touring bands, on subsequent albums and promotional material, he was always listed as a member of 'The Eagles Band'.

'Born to Boogie' (Henley/Frey/Felder/Schmit/Walsh) 2.16

Borrowing a title more commonly associated with Marc Bolan, this short ad-libbed jam was an outtake from *The Long Run* sessions. Frey sings vocal while the band do their best Canned Heat meets early ZZ Top impersonation. Bearing in mind what a miserable few months they spent recording the album, having fun with this must have come as a welcome spot of light relief to them. The compilation packaging gives no writing credits, though most online sources assign it to all five members. One names Hank Williams Jr. as the writer, though his 'Born to Boogie' was released in 1987 and is clearly a different song.

'The Long Run Leftovers' (Walsh/Henley/Frey/Felder/Schmit) 3.02

A selection of instrumental demos, presumably intended as intros, breaks or possibly as ideas for brand new songs, all in different tempi and rhythms, spliced together as one.

'Random Victims, Part 3' (Walsh/Henley/Frey/Felder/Meisner/ Schmit) 9.42

Not really a bonus track so much as an assortment of pieces of conjoined tomfoolery in the studio. As both Meisner and Schmit are credited as co-writers (or creators, rather), these remnants were presumably from tapes left running during sessions for the last two albums. 'Welcome to another episode of Random Victims', a voice announces early on, followed by several minutes of dialogue (sample: 'Excuse me, fartheads, I'm trying to fix my snare drum'), singing along very badly to the intro of 'Hotel California', and a few seconds of 'The Last Resort', sending it up with daft lyrics, brief extracts from 'Pretty Maids All in a Row' and 'Teenage Jail', impersonations of cartoon characters and the like. One way to fill up the last few spare minutes on a CD, if nothing else.

Nine of the twelve songs from the New Year's Eve gig had previously been released by Eagles, seven on the previous studio albums, plus both sides of the 1978 Christmas single. There are subtle differences in some of these. 'Funky New Year' is rather tighter than the slapdash B-side recording, with a sax break followed by a rap about how they broke up, got back together, repeated several times, and sounds more like The Average White Band than anyone else. 'Take It to the Limit' features Frey on lead vocal, and those who expect the original's breathtaking high note during the final choruses will be disappointed. According to Felder, without Meisner's soulful voice, it simply didn't work. He had a point, for though Frey does an efficient enough job, his voice lacks the wistful, pleading quality that always made the original stand out. You can try and bottle magic a second time, but don't assume it will work. Still, the crowd are singing along, so it hardly matters. Their only really good number in the show, Felder opined, was a new R&B version of 'Best of My Love', taken at much the same tempo but with a sax intro that makes it less of a country rock tune. That leaves three other songs making their debut on an official Eagles release, two of them from Henley's greatest hits, plus an early Walsh tune.

'Dirty Laundry' (Henley/Danny Kortchmar) 5.54

The song that took its bow on Henley's first solo album, *I Can't Stand Still*, peaked at number three in America and number 59 in Britain in 1983. The targets of its wrath are the media, television and tabloid press coverage of sensationalist or negative news; 'kick 'em when they're up, kick 'em when they're down', rather than focus on important issues; 'we all know that crap is king'. It was written partly from personal experience after an incident when an underage call girl was found naked at his house, having overdosed on drugs, following a party.

Walsh and Schmit both played on the original recording. On this live version, Walsh and Felder both share in ferocious guitar breaks on a funky workout that is otherwise largely driven by a brisk beat and simple keyboard riff.

'Funk #49' (Walsh/Jim Fox/Dale Peters) 3.47

From disco to hard rock, as Walsh resurrects a tune from his distant past. 'Funk #49' was a minor hit in 1970 and also a track on *James Gang Rides Again*, the second album from a power trio that was his band of 30 years earlier. What few lyrics there are mean little, being about a high-spirited lady friend. Most of it is instrumental, being built around one of his patent guitar licks – as was the lyrically deeper 'Life in the Fast Lane' about six years later.

'All She Wants To Do Is Dance (Danny Kortchmar) 5.20

Henley's apparent dislike of disco didn't stop him from dipping a toe in the genre when it came to looking for hits in the 1980s; and he could at least maintain that he was using it to put across a serious message. Funk-laden keyboard riffs drive this dancefloor-friendly blast at the hedonism of teens and twenty-somethings who seemingly care more for a night on the town, strutting their stuff, instead of paying any heed to the iniquities of their government's domestic and foreign policy – or as the old cliché says, fiddling while Rome burned. How much the intended targets of his anger took the message on board as they cheerfully bopped the night away is open to question, but what can be heard of the ecstatic audience reaction as the song starts suggest that they were more preoccupied about partying like it's 1999 than getting angry with the policies of their president. Once again, a pulsating beat with guitar, keyboards and sax all rising to the occasion demonstrate that Eagles could still make everyone dance until they dropped.

21st-century Eagles

By the time Eagles celebrated the 30th anniversary of their initial formation, the record industry had changed beyond recognition. As Henley told a reporter in the *Herald Sun* in October 2001, in common with many other acts, they didn't have a contract any longer. In future, they would go down the path of forming their own company, making records with their own money, issuing it themselves and maintaining full control.

A few weeks earlier, at the end of August, they were feeling fully refreshed after completing a tour of Europe on which they had played their first-ever dates in Italy, Finland and Russia. On 10 September, they were in Los Angeles, looking forward to entering the studios next morning to begin further recording sessions. Then the 9/11 news broke across a shocked universe; they contacted each other, and agreed that work was the last thing on their minds.

'Hole in the World' (Henley/Frey) 4.17

Having allowed the news of the Twin Towers attacks that morning to sink in, at his home studio that evening, Henley sat down at his piano and played around with a few chords based on the phrase 'hole in the world'. A refrain and first verse followed quickly, and then writer's block set in. He didn't show his work to anybody for a few months when other events brought additional meaning to the title. To him, their involvement in the Iraq war was particularly disquieting, with more people being killed in the Middle East every day even though the fighting was officially over. For everybody affected with a loved one not coming home, it meant another hole in their life.

> There are holes in the information that the public is getting, both from the media and the government. There are holes in what passes for the logic of this administration's foreign policy. The stars and stripes may be flying and the drums beating, but things are never going to be the same for some people. The ill-conceived attempt to 'avenge' the victims of September 11 has only brought more misery and sorrow. Things in today's world are not so black-and-white, so clear-cut. This is not a John Wayne movie. This is the 21st century.

He took his unfinished piece to the studio and showed it to Frey, who wrote the second verse. Between them, they started a third verse and then scrapped it in favour of keeping it simpler. At first, he had thought of it as a very short song, like some of the short pieces The Beatles recorded towards the end of their career together on side two of *Abbey Road*, about a minute in duration each.

The stark simplicity is effective. It's like a gospel song, with the chorus a chant, two verses (Henley taking lead vocal) asking how blind people can be and how mankind will never reach the promised land 'until we learn to love one another'. A modulation nearly halfway through brings further choruses, one sung against a reprise against the first verse and another sung a cappella until the fade. Guitars, Hammond organ, pianos and the rhythm section are all used with great restraint.

Despite their passionately held views on the war, Henley made it clear that none of the band intended to follow the example of The Dixie Chicks or Santana by making any statements in public during their overseas concerts. They would perform the song onstage but maintained that their audiences were not coming 'to hear polemics'.

The first record to appear on the new Eagles Recording Co. label, it was released as a CD single in 2003 in Britain, America, Europe and Australia in various formats, some including a live version as well as the studio recording, plus DVDs. It peaked at number 69 in America in July and at the same position in Britain in October.

At the same time, yet another compilation appeared in the form of *Complete Greatest Hits*, a 33-track double CD spanning their career from 1972 to the present, with 'Get Over It', 'Love Will Keep Us Alive', and 'Hole in the World' supplementing the 1970s classics. It went Top 10 on both sides of the Atlantic, with a peak of number three in America and number nine in Britain.

Recordings from shows over three nights at the Rod Laver Arena, Melbourne, Australia, in November 2004 yielded a double DVD released one year later, *Farewell 1 Tour – Live from Melbourne*. Frey explained the title by saying that the longer their tour continued, the better the songs sounded to them. They considered there was a kind of non-committal honesty 'in calling the tour Farewell 1, with its implication that Farewell 2 will follow soon'. Their first live video as a quartet without Felder, it found them accompanied by four other backing musicians, namely Steuart Smith, Michael Thompson and Will Hollis, both on keyboards, and Scott Crago on drums. Among the 30 songs were two brand new numbers, Walsh's 'One Day At A Time', which would appear on his next solo set *Analog Man*, and Frey's 'No More Cloudy Days'. The latter, plus two more exclusives, 'Do Something' and 'Fast Company', were first released in 2006 on a bonus audio CD of a special edition exclusive to Walmart, as a sampler for the new album that some had wondered might never arrive. But everyone's patience was ultimately rewarded.

Long Road Out of Eden (2007)

Personnel:
Glenn Frey: vocals, guitars, keyboards, bass guitar
Don Henley: vocals, drums, percussion, guitars
Joe Walsh: vocals, guitars, keyboards
Timothy B. Schmit: vocals, bass guitar
Additional personnel:
Steuart Smith: guitar, keyboards, mandolin
Scott Crago: drums, percussion
Richard F.W. Davis: keyboards, programming
Michael Thompson: keyboards, accordion, trombone
Will Hollis: keyboards
Al Garth: alto saxophone, violin
Bill Armstrong: trumpet
Chris Mostert: tenor and alto saxophone
Greg Smith: baritone saxophone
Greg Leisz: pedal steel guitar
Lenny Castro, Luis Conte: percussion
Orchestrations: Richard F.W. Davis, Glenn Frey
Horns arranged by Greg Smith and Don Henley
Produced by Eagles, Steuart Smith, Richard F.W. Davis, Scott Crago and Bill Szymczyk
Recorded at The Doghouse, Los Angeles, California; Samhain Sound, Malibu, California; O'Henry Sound Studios, Burbank, California; Henson Recording Studios, Hollywood, California; Moose Lodge, Calabasas, California; The Panhandle House, Denton, Texas; Luminous Sound, Dallas, Texas
Record label: Eagles Recording Co./Universal
Release date: October 2007
Highest chart positions: 1 (UK); 1 (US)
Running time: 90:46

Eagles' first all-studio album for 28 years had a long period of gestation, having been recorded in spurts over five or six years with one or two tracks possibly started or at least envisaged well before that, when Felder was still a member. Szymczyk was created as a co-producer, but by this time, he had largely become what Henley called 'a mediator, a consigliere, a ringmaster', and had handed on the torch to him and Frey. Steuart Smith, Richard F.W. Davis and Scott Crago were now part of 'The Eagles Band', with their names appearing in a lower paragraph on the credits and their pictures nowhere to be seen in the booklet or on the artwork. For the first time ever, the lyrics to all songs were included.

The band did most of their work on the album separately, using digital file transfer for the first time. It led to suggestions that the record was, in part, a batch of members' solo tracks gathered together and issued as a band album for the sake of convenience. Moreover, even with these technological advances of allowing them to function remotely, it was still a mammoth task, having taken about six years to complete. But at last, they were in a position to take their time without management holding them to deadlines.

Despite the individual projects in addition to *Hell Freezes Over* during the 28-year break that separated this from *The Long Run*, it was not surprising that they had enough material between them for a double album. Henley had mixed feelings, telling *Billboard* that he, for one would have preferred it to be a single collection and would have gone about it a little differently, omitting a couple of songs, for instance. But the rest thought otherwise – 'we vote by committee'.

In retrospect, some reviewers said that the first disc sounded more like an Eagles album, very much a successor to their country rock sound of the early days that, at length, they seemed to be trying to distance themselves from. The second one seemed to some ears to have been more dominated by Henley, 'a bit like an Eagles lost album from the Reagan years', and closer to how his next solo album would have turned out had they not joined forces again for *Long Road Out of Eden*. On a casual listen, it sounds mellow, despite the weighty subject matter of some of the lyrics. Walsh is not really playing guitar with the force he did in his younger days, mainly as the style of the songs hardly demands it, and the lack of Felder's 'heir to Duane Allman' playing certainly leaves a gap. It also strikes one as odd that Smith, who was recruited to replace Felder, is not credited as a full member of the band yet receives four co-writing credits against Walsh's two, one of the latter being an old song initially planned for a different project altogether.

There were bonus tracks for the UK and US editions, 'Hole in the World' for the former, 'Please Come Home for Christmas' on the latter. A deluxe collector's edition, including both, was issued in red linen cloth, screen printed with panoramic imagery, with a 40-page booklet including lyrics and credits (which were also in the 20-page booklet packaged with the standard edition), exclusive photos and desert scenes from the making of the 'How Long' video.

For the first year of release, it was available in North America exclusively via the band's own website, Walmart and Sam's Club retail stores, and it became the first account-exclusive album to reach number one. The record was released on their own label, Eagles Recording Co., through Lost Highway in America and through Polydor in Europe, both part of Universal Music Group. As they now had their own label, there was no deadline – until an increasingly impatient Walmart, having been advised that it was coming together at long last, urged them to complete it in time for the Christmas season.

The band's decision to sell the album exclusively by a company not widely respected for its business practices caused some adverse comment, especially as that company had previously refused to supply music it considered controversial. Henley admitted that he didn't like big-box retailers, and his own father had been a small businessman. But times had changed and the deal enabled them to receive a larger portion of the profits than one offered by a standard record deal, basically cutting out the record company middleman. They were in the business of selling records, and having formed their own record label, were in a position to negotiate a royalty that no standard record company could offer them. For them, it was the best deal they could get at a time when most music fans were getting their music free from streaming services and many record shops were closing their doors. Henley said that Walmart couldn't be any more evil than a major record label.

Critical reactions to the record itself were inevitably mixed. In *Rolling Stone*, David Fricke singled out the title track for the greatest praise, saying that 'the ten-minute centerpiece epitomises everything that is familiar, surprising, overstretched and, in many ways, right about the entire set ... a bargain even with the misfires, worth it for the title song alone.' For *Record Collector*, Terry Staunton found it 'a mixed bag, highlighting the band's strengths and exposing their occasional soft-option weaknesses'. Chris Jones' BBC Review called it 'an album played with verve, filled with lyrical incisiveness and still retaining the warm smell of colitas, whatever they are'. For *Slant*, Jonathan Keefe said it proved they were 'still commercially relevant', even if he couldn't resist calling the album 'calculated, tepid', and saying it was 'not likely to influence another generation of musicians'. The most scathing comment came from Jude Rogers of *The Guardian,* who was unimpressed, awarding it one star out of five and writing that while self-importance might be a given in the world of soft rock, the band's comeback 'propels musical smugness to previously inconceivable proportions ... At least the album provides a thousand unintentional laughs as it takes awfulness to new heights.' *Classic Rock* admitted that it had 'far-flung highlights' like the title track but opined that it shifted too often 'between bleak acceptance and schoolmarm scolding' and was 'simply too long'.

Nevertheless, consumer reaction was all that they could have wished for in proving how eagerly it had been awaited. It topped the album charts in the first week of release in America, their sixth to achieve the summit, and in Britain, where it was their first to do so.

Frey was particularly proud of what they had achieved, and though he stopped short of calling it their best-ever, he told *Billboard* that he thought it was ...

... going to be right up there, if you want to know the truth. If you look back on our previous albums of the 1970s, those albums are four or five songs deep, and you can just about name them off of each album. You can name the three smash hit singles and then one or two album cuts that were essential to the record. This record is like 15 songs deep, and the other thing that I am really heartened by is that the quality of the recording is so much better now. I think the production level is far superior.

There was a return to their early days in that, like the first album, the front cover photograph was shot in the California desert, this time with an image of the sun setting over empty dunes. On the back, the band were seen outside Los Angeles by Olaf Heine in March 2007, wandering the same sands in the 'How Long' video. The photography was by Olaf Heine, with Jeri Heiden responsible for art direction and design.

'No More Walks In The Wood' (Henley/Steuart Smith/John Hollander) 2.00

A prelude to the album, this short song uses the words from 'An Old-Fashioned Song', a 21-line poem without choruses either in poem or song by one of the most noted poets and literary critics of the age. Hollander had published it in a collection of verse in 1993. On reading it, Henley decided it would make an excellent short song, and was accordingly given permission to set it to music with the aid of guitarist Steuart. The band sing it in four-part harmony, mostly a cappella, with occasional acoustic guitar chords. This is in effect, their 'Seven Bridges Road' for the new century.

'How Long' (J.D. Souther) 3.15

Written by Souther in 1969, this was part of the band's regular repertoire when they performed it as part of their live sets in the early/mid-1970s, but didn't record it at the time as he was intending to use it on his first solo album in 1972. They included it in a performance at a Dutch pop gala in 1973, on a clip later uploaded to YouTube. Years later, Frey's children came across it, were much amused by the sight of their twenty-something father, and his wife Cindy told him they should record it for release.

Souther told *Rolling Stone* that the song was the tale of a soldier in the Vietnam War who went absent without leave, was caught and sentenced for murder. He asked his girlfriend how long she was prepared to wait for his release. There wasn't a happy ending as he never returned to her, though whether he died in prison, or was set free and found somebody else, is anyone's guess.

It was a smart move to include this on the album as a reminder of the country rock sound that had carved out their reputation in the early 1970s, and several reviewers picked it as the best song on the album. Very much in the style of 'Take It Easy' and 'Already Gone', it was another of their most instantly infectious songs ever (nobody can resist joining in with the chorus after hearing it a couple of times), a cheerful, upbeat three minutes that belies the sombre subject matter. Frey and Henley shared lead vocals on the verses, with an embarrassment of harmonies on the choruses and the closing verse.

In the download era, singles had become largely a promotional device for the media, as opposed to the mass marketing of physical discs available over the counter on high streets, with record retail outlets having become an increasingly endangered species. It was, however, released as a single to radio and TV in America in August 2007, small quantities of 7" vinyl copies with the song on both sides being circulated, and to the media soon afterwards in Britain, where it was playlisted by BBC Radio 2. Had it been a 7" vinyl single on general release two or three decades earlier, it would surely have been a Top 20 hit at least. According to *Billboard,* it made number 101 in America, and the Official Charts Company in Britain, number 110. (It may be of interest to the most ardent music trivia buffs that the latter body also records a chart position in Britain for 'Take It Easy' in 2013 when it reached number 188. Don't get too excited).

'Busy Being Fabulous' (Henley/Frey) 4.21

Henley takes the lead vocal on another 'witchy woman' – yes, the general tempo and mood recall that song from the 1972 debut album – with a misogynistic put-down in best sneering Mick Jagger tradition. The husband comes back to an empty house and finds a note from unfaithful wife, telling him not to wait up as she is out on the town living it up. She's 'just too busy being fabulous, instead of thinking about us', evidently in pursuit of her faded youth while she tries to behave like a woman half her age. At least she's not there for him to see a pair of lyin' eyes. A muscular guitar figure and organ dominate the arrangement.

'What Do I Do With My Heart' (Henley/Frey) 3.55

While Henley pours scorn on his other half in the previous song, Frey is more forgiving as he tells her how as she has found somebody better, he won't stand in her way, though he'd do anything to have her back. Frey's suitably soulful solo vocals lead on verse one, with classic Eagles harmonies on verse two, then an interesting interlude that breaks completely with the main melody, and an impassioned last verse that finds Frey mustering every bit of soul as he assures her he'll love her till death parts them both. Restrained guitar, keyboards and rhythm section support well a song that it would be easy to knock as twee and soppy, but very effective nonetheless and would have been ripe for covering by many a country balladeer or crooner.

'Guilty of the Crime' (Frankie Miller/Jerry Lynn Williams) 3.44

After Henley and Frey dominate the first four tracks, Walsh steps up with some timely contrast on a song co-written by Scottish blues-rock singer Frankie Miller and the man called probably the most successful unknown songwriter in rock and rhythm and blues, Jerry Lynn Williams, who had written material for Eric Clapton, Bonnie Raitt and B.B. King.

Miller and Walsh had been friends for over thirty years, from the days when James Gang appeared on the same bill during the early 1970s and they developed great respect for each others' talents. In 1994 they met in New York to write and record material for a new band comprising them both, keyboard player Nicky Hopkins and former King Crimson drummer

Ian Wallace. One of the songs they completed was also planned for the soundtrack of the superhero movie *RoboCop* but was not used. Sadly the album was never completed, as in August of that year Miller was suddenly taken ill with a near-fatal haemorrhage that left him in a coma for several months. On regaining consciousness, he was unable to sing or even speak, and after more than a year in hospital he needed an intensive course of rehabilitation. The recording appeared with some other previously unreleased material on another Miller album, *Long Way Home,* in 2006. Aware that it was unlikely to attract many sales outside his dedicated fan base, Walsh decided to record it on the new album to ensure some well-deserved royalties for its co-writer. When they played a date at the Indigo Club at the O2 Arena in London at the start of their tour in March 2008, a wheelchair-bound Miller was in the audience. Walsh gave him a shout-out and the audience added a huge round of applause.

Walsh's growl comes close to matching Miller's exemplary bluesy vocal, with powerful slide guitar and pub-rock piano of the first order, capturing something of Rod Stewart and the Faces at their gloriously ramshackle best. It may not be the deepest track on the album, but it's undeniably one of the most fun.

The song was also previously recorded by The Bellamy Brothers on their 1997 album *Over the Line.* In 2009, they recorded a version with country rock band The Bacon Brothers and released it as a single.

'I Don't Want To Hear Any More' (Paul Carrack) 4.21

After 'I Can't Tell You Why' and 'Love Will Keep us Alive', Schmit had become the band's main balladeer. Following their unsuccessful attempt to form a band in the 1980s, he and Carrack had remained friends, and the latter gave him a demo of the song backstage after a gig in England. A smooth, soulful ballad in which the lyrics tell of coming to terms with the end of a love affair in which neither partner needs to tell the other that it's all over, the bassist delivers a flawless if perhaps slightly too sweet vocal, with harmonies from the others and a subdued guitars and keyboards backing. Carrack had also recorded a very similar arrangement of the song, with Schmit and Henley on backing vocals, which appeared on his subsequent solo album *I Know That Name* the following year.

'Waiting in the Weeds' (Henley/Steuart Smith) 7.47

The album's second longest track is among those that has often been hailed as one of Henley's masterpieces. Schmit called it 'a sweet song, really, a jewel of the album'. Is it a personal love song, as he waits for the object of his affections to realise that she has given her heart to the wrong man, feels hurt, and finds it impossible to move on?

Or is it a veiled lyric about how he says that on the band's getting back together again in 1994, they were older, more mature, had families of their own, intended to work at a slower pace in future, and with revised priorities?

When he was asked about what it meant, Henley said he had just turned 60 but wasn't complaining; he was thrilled and delighted. He hints that the latter scenario is a more likely one.

> None of us ever thought it would go on this long. But we are a determined bunch of guys. We take our time. We are not afraid of the passage of time, necessarily, and we've been sitting one out for a long time. That is kind of what 'Waiting in the Weeds' implies. Again, on the surface, that's a love song, but it's also about this band. We've just been sort of waiting for some of this bad music to die down, for certain trends to go away, so that we can get out there on the dance floor again. We are a band that knows how to bide its time, and how to wait.

One verse tells of 'biding time with the crows and sparrows, while peacocks prance and strut upon the stage.' If finding love is just a dance, proximity and chance, he continues, 'You will excuse me if I skip the masquerade.' It might be about waiting for love, waiting for his chance – or, as has been suggested, talking about manufactured pop puppets, untalented nine-day wonders of whom the public will tire quickly before the old bands who have stood the test of time are back in favour once more. How strongly he felt for or against younger musical artists is uncertain. In 2004 he lamented in an editorial in the *Washington Post* that the three largest music retailers – Best Buy, Walmart and Target – had limited shelf space, making it harder for new artists to emerge. Three years later, he said that if Eagles put out a record on Warner or any other major record label, part of the reason they couldn't pay a decent royalty was because 'we've got to pay for all of the bad acts they sign and release.'

There are allusions to not wishing to wait forever – 'And though I heard some wise man say that every dog will have his day, He never mentioned that these dog days get so long.' But then the references to love and romance recur; images and memories of sunlight in the loved one's hair at the county fair, holding hands and laughing, while the flavour of the week (the ice cream) is melting down her pretty summer dress. At the end comes an air of resignation – he has been keeping to himself, knowing the seasons are slowly changing; 'Even though you're with somebody else, he'll never love you like I do.' Let listeners make of it what they will.

Lyrically, the song has an unusual structure in that the chorus comes four times, with the second and third both featuring new lyrics, and only the last repeating the first. The musical arrangement is peerless, with touches of classical guitar on nylon strings, piano, mandolin and accordion in a hazy, gentle wash of sound.

'No More Cloudy Days' (Frey) 4.04

A pattern seems to be emerging as the sequence of songs continues. After a song by Henley that is either quite merciless in its targets or else enshrouded in metaphors and open to multiple interpretations and meanings, Frey counters it with a simple love song that has no hidden depths and merely looks forward to a brighter future. Over unobtrusive guitars and a relaxed rhythm section, he sings of sitting at a foggy window, looking out at the pouring rain, while he anticipates an improvement in the weather with happier times, 'no more stormy nights, no more cloudy days'.

'Fast Company' (Henley/Frey) 4.01

Keep throwing in the occasional musical surprise. Play this to someone who's hearing it for the first time, and after hearing a tune dominated by Henley's uncharacteristic falsetto, they'd probably say it was a partnership between Prince and Stevie Wonder. It's more or less the closest to funk they ever got on any of their studio albums, although rather slower than 'Life in the Fast Lane', and instead of being built on a swaggering guitar riff, is framed around the strutting beat that powered Henley's 'Dirty Laundry', with horns and organ taking over for the last minute. Henley and Frey said they wrote this for their small daughters as a kind of cautionary tale about how vulnerable they can be to peer pressure, and the passion to be liked. It's fine to have some fun; the last verse tells them, your life has just begun, and you can't get away, but keep your feet on the ground, and be careful about running with the fast company.

'Do Something' (Henley/Frey/Schmit) 5.13

A gentle lullaby-like number led by acoustic guitar and with a pedal steel joining in softly later behind Schmit's vocal, this is a song that could have come from one of the band's earlier albums. Henley, who sings the bridge, commented that it was partly a love song but also inspired by his childhood days. If somebody was feeling down, the remedy was to 'do something' instead of indulging in self-pity or seeking therapy and support groups, or stop complaining and try to fix the problem yourself. Everything you believed in has been turned upside down, the whole world's gone crazy, you pick up the morning paper and there's nothing but bad news. It's a rather more soothing sequel to 'Get Over It' from *Hell Freezes Over*.

'You Are Not Alone' (Frey) 2.22

Something of the comforting message of Carole King's' You've Got a Friend', and the folksy acoustic guitar and harmonica intro of Ralph McTell's 'Streets of London', permeate this short but charming one-man effort by Frey. He wrote this for his daughter during a particularly troubled time in her childhood.

'Long Road Out of Eden' (Henley/Frey/Schmit) 10.17

The longest track they ever released is a startling epic, a kind of 'Hotel California' some 30 years on, but this time extending its horizons beyond the state of contemporary America in the wake of the 9/11 attacks and looking at its general position in the 21st century, vis-à-vis foreign policy under the presidency of George W. Bush and the protracted, seemingly never-ending stalemate of wars in Iraq and Afghanistan in the Middle East. Rich in metaphor, biblical allusions and references to ancient history, it is studded with lines and pithy observations that would repay an appearance in any dictionary of modern quotations.

Iraq and Afghanistan are not specifically mentioned, but the implication is clear. The Garden of Eden is commonly reckoned to be in southern Mesopotamia, now Iraq. Meanwhile, a complacent America believes that the nation is riding to Utopia and, according to the road map, will be arriving soon. Little do they realise that they're walking or struggling on a long, seemingly interminable road out of Eden. Captains of the old order are clinging to the reins – one assumes these are either the politicians or the captains of industry, as opposed to the military commanders close to the front line. They're at home, rolling down the interstate, lunching at their clubs with their fine cigars to look forward to afterwards. Meanwhile, on the other side of the world are the 'poor bloody infantry', the soldiers in the desert doing the politicians' dirty work and risking their lives, barely recognising the region's historical significance, wondering why they are there in the first place, not counting on still being there tomorrow – and they can't tell wrong from right. All they know is that they'd rather be back at home in the arms of their loved ones tonight.

Some of the song deals with the way information is disseminated in modern times, and (as in 'The Last Resort') Henley's anger in the last verse is palpable. Breathless cable news anchors and clickbait internet stories have taken the place of nuanced coverage, and more than ever, it's driven by moneyed interests. Now everyone is ...

Weavin' down the American highway
Through the litter and the wreckage and the cultural junk
Bloated with entitlement, loaded on propaganda
Now we're drivin' dazed and drunk.

While he may not have explained everything in his lyrics in detail, preferring to leave others to work it out for themselves and perhaps look forward to a chuckle at some of the more imaginative interpretations, on this one he was quite explicit. He told *Billboard* that he had originally intended to write 'weaving down the information highway' because (like everyone else) he went on his computer every day and, as with television, was exasperated by the surfeit of nonsense online. 'In the end, I decided that it wouldn't make a lot of sense with the rest of the song just to suddenly go over and start talking about computers and the internet. So I changed it back to American highway just to make it broader in scope.' The implication is that, to use a cliché, nobody can really see their way when confronted with an excess of 'cultural junk'.

He – for that, read the average American – has been down the road to Damascus, signifying a startling turning point or change in attitude after a wake-up call. Next, he has met the ghost of Caesar on the Appian Way, the Roman road of classical times that was used as the main route for carrying military supplies, where he is told that 'the road to empire is a bloody stupid waste'. His most damning statement is left till last; 'All the knowledge in the world is of no use to fools.'

On a musical level, this lyric of epic proportions receives the painstaking arrangement for which it cries out. The minute-long intro is a concise but potent soundscape of chilling desert winds and an eastern wind instrument, both joined by a bell tolling in the background. Then the warm tones of an electric piano lead into the first verse, with acoustic guitar joining in as Henley paints an atmospheric picture in words of the moon shining down the palms, while shadows move on the sands and a soldier with a dusty rifle in his hands whispers the words of the 23rd Psalm, as if seeking comfort and protection in a hostile land.

Throughout the song, the vocal harmonies, acoustic guitar keyboards and an eerie lead guitar break enhance the song with restraint, with occasional peaks in a few sparing, crashing electric guitar chords about five minutes in, and a military drumbeat in the last minute before guitars fade into the howling wind at the end. It may have been too long, and too devoid of any instantly recognisable hook, to become another 'Stairway to Heaven' or 'Won't Get Fooled Again', beloved by classic rock radio from time to time. But at the risk of stating the obvious, it all adds up to a striking, complex ten minutes of words and music.

'I Dreamed There Was No War' (Frey) 1.38
The shortest track on the album follows the longest, like a brief coda. A gently picked acoustic guitar bedded by lush orchestration evokes the same kind of musical landscape as some of Mark Knopfler's film music, notably 'Going Home'.

'Somebody' (Jack Tempchin/John Brannen) 4.10
This could have come from, and was a possible leftover from, Frey's solo work of the 1980s. A full-blooded intro of a guitar twang, backed by organ and drums, instantly brings songs like 'Born to Run' and 'Atomic' to mind on one of the album's most instantly commercial moments. Add to that another spiky guitar solo, presumably Walsh's work. The lyric is addressed to someone who has led a life of infamy but is now on the run and about to pay for his misdeeds. A chilling last verse sums up images of the miscreant who is about to die beneath a moon in the midnight sky while a big black crow perched on a tombstone in the graveyard is calling him home – sung in Frey's most mocking tones.

'Frail Grasp on the Big Picture' (Henley/Frey) 5.47

Henley takes the vocal on one of his most angry songs yet. To a rhythm that recalls the Rolling Stones' more funk-driven experiments of the 1970s and 1980s, his lyrics lambast the ignorance and arrogance of Middle America on political and cultural issues. His fellow countrymen, he rants, have short memories, never learn from history, and keep making the same mistakes. The light's fading, the fog's getting thicker, they're heading for the dark ages ... In other words, it's a despairing assertion that real journalism and debate are dead because opinion leaders assume they know it all. Three minutes in, the backing track cuts out to be replaced by the warm sound of a church organ, as he intones how 'we pray to our Lord who we know is American'. He reigns from on high, supports us in war, presides over football games, and the right will prevail.

There are some who regard it as ill-tempered, world-weary condescension, and some who will take such irony seriously, but it's safer to assume that he's poking fun at the humourless, xenophobic elements who believe that they are always unassailably correct. We have faith in the Lord – unless there's money or sex involved. There are elements here of a 21st-century reiteration of the young Bob Dylan's refrain from one of his early songs, 'With God on our Side', reflecting the unshakeable belief of the American conservative right, 'the land that I live in has God on its side.'

'Last Good Time in Town' (Walsh/J.D. Souther) 7.08

Walsh's second vocal and the only one he co-wrote (his verses, Souther's chorus) came almost three decades after his first sardonic memoir in 'Life's Been Good'. In contrast to Henley's polemics and Frey's odes to fatherhood and family life, their guitarist now savours the simple pleasures of staying behind his own front door – doing the crossword, turning off the phone, closing the curtains, even playing his trombone, while he leaves the partying lifestyle to others. It's an easy-going, relaxed concept that deserves and is set to a relaxed musical framework, with a percussion intro and Latin feel that sounds like he's hooked up with Carlos Santana and band. A leisurely, if slightly overlong, guitar break and a few trombone toots flesh the song out in appropriate style.

'I Love to Watch a Woman Dance' (Larry John McNally) 3.16

American songwriter McNally (not to be confused with John McNally of British 1960s favourites The Searchers) wrote this while he was visiting a music club in Amsterdam and was captivated by watching a room swirling with dancers to the music of a gypsy band. He sent it to Henley after the latter had recorded another of his songs, 'For my Wedding', on his solo album *Inside Job*, released in 2000. They had expressed interest and begun work on it during the abortive late 1990s band sessions. In McNally's words, 'eight years went by before it was released with zero communication from the band'. Having been alternately hopeful that they would use it and then in despair, in July 2007, he heard a bootleg recording of Frey singing it at a solo gig, saying it might be on the forthcoming album, and when he heard the finished result, he said it was 'done very nicely'. Performed as a waltz, Frey brings out the melody beautifully with lightly picked guitars, lush harmonies and accordion.

'Business as Usual' (Henley/Steuart Smith) 5.32
Another song that sounds influenced by 1980s-era Rolling Stones, this combines mid-tempo rock verging on funk with a tune built mostly on minor chords. Henley rants about greed and corruption, leading to complacency about the quality of life and lack of environmental concern, those who 'worship at the marketplace', how 'monuments to arrogance reach for the sky' and 'our better nature's buried in the rubble'. He told *Rolling Stone* that it was his commentary on the general collective unconsciousness, how people went about day in day out, quite oblivious to or simply not concerned about the bigger picture. 'How naive we are about the inner workings and the destructive forces of big business and politics, the irreversible damage that's being done to the planet and so many of its voiceless inhabitants.' Some figured that he might be pointing the finger at Eagles themselves: 'A barrel of monkeys, a band of renown'.

'Center of the Universe' (Henley/Frey/Steuart Smith) 3.42
Having seemingly satisfied his quota of social comment, Henley goes sentimental with a lovelorn ballad, imploring his loved one through a 'veil of tears' for understanding. Framed neatly by acoustic guitars, touches of accordion and strings, it also includes a short break wreathed in ethereal vocal harmonies, fronted by a lightly picked nylon-stringed guitar played so delicately that the sound of fingers moving up the strings are audible at one point.

'It's Your World Now' (Frey/Jack Tempchin) 4.20
There is a sense of finality in the lyrics to what is surely the most moving song on the album, like a more contemporary 'My Way'; 'My race is run, I'm moving on, like the setting sun, no sad goodbyes, no tears allowed.' Now a contented family man in his fifties with three young children, Frey writes and sings to them of how he is passing on the torch to the next generation. Yet again, it's another acoustic ballad, but this time with a relaxed mariachi setting of Mexican trumpets behind the guitars.

Henley was particularly taken with this song, which he called his musical partner's 'beautiful valediction' to his wife and their children. For him, the focus of it was the lines: 'Be part of something good, leave something good behind.' It summed up everything for him as well as for Frey, 'to my children, to my fans, to everybody. If there was one message to this album that I want to impart, that would be it.'

When Frey died in January 2016, Eagles posted the lyrics of the song alongside the announcement of his death on their website. 'Words can neither describe our sorrow nor our love and respect for all that he has given to us, his family, the music community & millions of fans worldwide.'

'Hole in the World' (Henley/Frey) 4.17 – UK bonus track [see 21st Century Eagles chapter]
'Please Come Home For Christmas' (Charles Mose Brown/Gene C. Redd) – US bonus track [see Exit Meisner, Enter Schmit chapter]

Would there be another album?

Henley was not slow to give the impression that *Long Road Out of Eden* had marked the conclusion of their work together as a band, in the studio at least. 'It's almost as if we knew that record would be our last,' he told *Rolling Stone*, soon after release. To CNN, he said that while it was not for him to say that there would never be another, he pointed out that it contained 20 songs, and they got a lot of things off their chest. 'I don't know if anybody's going to want to do another one.' Later he seemed to be having second thoughts, telling CBS News that there might be more. Making new records was 'addictive, and you wanna keep doing it'. But almost 30 years earlier, while they were painfully recording *The Long Run*, he had gone on record as saying he'd like to make a really great studio album, perhaps a double, and then 'go out gracefully'. This was evidently the one he was referring to.

Just like old times, the band went out on the road to promote the album. The Long Road Out of Eden tour started with four dates in March 2008, at London's O2 Arena, across the world and finally winding up with two dates at the MGM Grand Garden Arena, Las Vegas, in November 2011. Nine of the tracks off the new album were featured regularly on the tour, with 'How Long' not surprisingly being the most frequently played.

Two other members of the band gave separate interviews around 2010, speculating on the chances of a (or another?) final album. Schmit admitted that bands were a fragile entity, and it was impossible for anyone to predict what would happen. Walsh was of a similar mind, not committing himself but leaving the idea on the table. They might make one more before the band 'wraps it up'.

Six years later, they were 'wrapping it up' in a different sense, with *History of the Eagles*, an authorised two-part documentary first shown as a feature film, then aired on television and released on DVD in 2013. It was supported by a tour of the same name, from July 2013 to July 2015, covering North America, Europe and Oceania. Leadon was welcomed back into the line-up, and Meisner was invited to join them but had to decline because of ill health. Felder was still *persona non grata*.

The tour came just in time for Frey, for he had been unwell for some time with arthritis and an inflammatory disorder. Little did they know that their gig on 29 July 2015 at Bossier City, Louisiana, was to be the last he ever played. Prescribed medication led to colitis and pneumonia, and though he was able to fulfil all the contracted dates, they would be his public farewell. Admitted to hospital for major surgery later that year, he died in January 2016, aged 67. One month later, the rest of the band played 'Take It Easy' as a tribute to him at the Grammy Awards, with Jackson Browne standing in on lead vocal, and subsequently at a private memorial with guest singers, including Frey's younger son, Deacon. Henley, the last original member of the line-up, said it was surely the last time they would play together. Glenn Frey had been the founding member of the band, and they simply felt they couldn't go on without him. They were sure the fans wouldn't accept anything else, and they just 'drifted' into a year of mourning.

Once again, Irving Azoff proved to be the catalyst. As ever, he was loath to see them leave the stage for the last time. After a break that might have been indefinite, he suggested that Vince Gill, who had a long and successful career as a country singer-songwriter, should join the line-up so they could go back on tour. As a long-term fan of the band and also as a former golfing buddy of Glenn Frey, he had performed at the Kennedy Center Honours in December 2016 when Eagles were honoured in recognition of their contributions to American culture. Henley was uncertain at first, but he believed that the band had a future if there was still family blood in the line-up. Once the possibility of recruiting Deacon Frey and Gill became a probability, everything fell into place. Two gigs at Classic West and Classic East festivals in Los Angeles and New York with the new line-up in the spring of 2017 were rapturously received by the audiences. That was all the encouragement they needed to continue, confident that the demand was still there.

When Robert Plant went on record as saying that Eagles only reformed because they were bored, Henley swiftly denied the charge. In an interview with Elif Ozden of Rock Celebrities, he explained that they enjoyed doing it, while conceding that it was hard work, especially for people of their age, but nonetheless a fantastic job, a wonderful way to make a living, see the world, get to travel and take the children with them. As Led Zeppelin were one of the greatest bands of all time, he really wished they would get back together, but thought Plant was worried about hitting those notes. 'He may not be able to unbutton his shirt anymore.'

That same year, they recorded 'Part of the Plan', a song by Dan Fogelberg, as one track on the *Tribute to Dan Fogelberg* album, to their old singer-songwriter friend who had died in 2007 after a three-year battle with cancer. Some of them had played sessions on his albums, and they had seriously considered inviting him to join the band in the early days.

As for the chances of any follow-up to *Long Road Out of Eden*, the odds were shortening. In 2018, by which time they were still touring, although the three remaining members of the late 1970s line-up had reached the age of 70, it was looking less likely than ever. When Henley was asked that year about the possibility of any more studio albums, he said he wasn't sure if he cared any more. 'We could make the best album we've ever made in the history of this band,' he told Dave Everley of *Classic Rock*, 'and it wouldn't get played on the radio simply because it's all about demographics now; it's about marketing youth to youth.' Walsh put it more succinctly. 'There are no albums. The internet ate 'em. There is no side two. If we made new music, it would be for us.'

Henley insisted that modern technology had impacted negatively on the music industry, especially with the proliferation of illegal sampling by younger DJs and others of older material. Rewriting the lyrics to somebody else's songs, recording it and putting it on the internet, he told Sean Michaels of *The Guardian*, was wrong. The new generation had grown up in a world that didn't understand or respect copyright material or intellectual property. 'They look at songs as interactive playthings.' But it didn't mean that their creative urge was gone forever. Some days he had it, Henley admitted; some days he didn't, as it comes and goes. 'One of the primary motivations of creating this stuff is that you know somebody's going to hear it. The point is to reach people. But it's just not there.' Over the years, the songs they had written and recorded already, comprising their back catalogue, had taken on a life of their own.

> We are only curating them. We are just the vehicle for presenting these songs to the people. We've come to realise what these songs mean to people, and how they're part of their lives. You could call it nostalgia, and there's nothing terrible about that comment, especially in times like these, when things are so unhinged and crazy.

Eager to prove he still had more numbers inside him, Henley released a fifth solo album, his second since Eagles reformed in 1994, in 2015. *Cass County,* featuring four songs he had co-written with Steuart Smith (one of which also credited Schmit as co-writer), was his most successful ever in terms of peak chart positions, becoming his first top-three American album and the first to reach the British Top ten. While it could hardly be called another Eagles record, Smith, Vince Gill and Richard Davis all appeared on it as singers or session musicians alongside guest artists, including Mick Jagger, Alison Krauss and Dolly Parton.

Even if the world had seen their last studio record, there would always be a place for another live album from the band.

Eagles Live from The Forum – MMXVIII (2020)

Personnel:
Don Henley: vocals, drums, guitar, percussion
Joe Walsh: vocals, guitar, keyboards
Timothy B. Schmit: vocals, bass guitar
Vince Gill: vocals, guitar
Deacon Frey: vocals, guitar
Additional personnel (listed as Eagles Band):
Steuart Smith: guitar, vocals
Will Hollis: keyboards, musical director
Michael Thompson: keyboards, accordion, trombone
Scott Crago: drums, percussion
Horns:
Michael Boscarino
Michael Cottone
Tom Evans
Jamie Hovorka
David Mann
Strings:
Milo Deering
Kristine Kruta
Christiana Liberis
Laura Sacks
Erica Swindell
Produced by Don Henley
Recorded at The Forum, Inglewood, Los Angeles, CA, 12, 14, 15 September 2018
Mixed at Sonic Boom, Blackbird Studios, Henson Studios
Mastered at Gateway Mastering
Record label: Eagles Recording Co./Rhino/Warner Bros
Release date: October 2020
Highest chart positions: 26 (UK); 16 (US)
Running time: 2:17:33
Tracklisting: 'Seven Bridges Road' (Steve Young); 'Take It Easy'; 'One of These Nights'; 'Take It to the Limit'; 'Tequila Sunrise'; 'In the City'; 'I Can't Tell You Why'; 'New Kid in Town'; 'How Long'; 'Peaceful Easy Feeling'; 'Ol' 55'; 'Lyin' Eyes'; 'Love Will Keep Us Alive'; 'Don't Let Our Love Start Slippin' Away' (Vince Gill/Pete Wasner); 'Those Shoes'; 'Already Gone'; 'Walk Away' (Walsh); 'Life's Been Good'; 'The Boys of Summer' (Henley/Mike Campbell); 'Heartache Tonight'; 'Funk #49'; 'Life in the Fast Lane'; 'Hotel California'; 'Rocky Mountain Way' (Walsh/Roche Grace/Kenny Passarelli/Joe Vitale); 'Desperado'; 'The Long Run'

The North American tour included three nights in September 2018 at the Forum, where the concerts were recorded for the CD and a concert film. Deacon assumed the mantle left him by his father, as did Vince Gill, on

another live album and what might possibly be destined to remain the last new official release in a catalogue stretching back almost half a century. Distilled from three concerts in California, this serves up performances of most of the greatest hits, a few album tracks, plus highlights from the solo careers of Henley, Walsh and Gill. It might be noted that there is only one song from *Long Road Out of Eden*, the old stage favourite from their early days, 'How Long'. Like his father, Frey sang lead on that, sharing verses with Henley, and on 'Take It Easy', and 'Already Gone', although on the latter, they omitted the key change from G to C on the 1973 original. Gill took lead on his own 'Don't Let Our Love Start Slippin' Away', as well as 'Take It to the Limit' (with those peerless high notes in the final choruses restored), 'Ol' 55', 'Lyin' Eyes', and 'Heartache Tonight'. 'Tequila Sunrise' benefits from an accordion in the backing. Meisner was in the audience one night, and Schmit gave his fondly remembered predecessor a call-out from the stage, resulting in a massive cheer from the audience.

'Don't Let Our Love Start Slippin' Away' (Vince Gill/Pete Wasner) 5.18

Gill never had a hit single or album on the national charts in Britain or America. Yet in his homeland, he had long been a well-respected country soloist, and at one stage, he was invited by Mark Knopfler, an admirer of his work, to join Dire Straits. This, a single for him in 1992, was one of his most successful on the US hot country chart, and became a regular fixture of Eagles' set once he had joined. It follows the original closely, although, with the band, it packs more of a punch on the guitar break.

'Walk Away' (Walsh) 3.58

Originally a minor American hit in 1971, peaking at number 51 for Walsh's first major band The James Gang, like 'Funk #49', this was regarded as one of the seminal fusions of funk, soul and heavy metal. With lyrics about the end of a relationship where the man is obviously reluctant to break it off while the woman just wants to 'turn [her] pretty head and walk away', the original was a powerful showcase for his early work. A little later, it found a regular place on Eagles' setlist, now enhanced with a brass section.

'The Boys of Summer' (Henley/Mike Campbell) 5.15

Henley's major solo success of the mid-1980s had started life as a demo created by Mike Campbell, guitarist with Tom Petty and the Heartbreakers, on a drum machine. They decided it would not work for them, so Campbell passed it to Henley, who wrote lyrics for it about coming to terms with middle age. Its most well-remembered line, about 'a Deadhead sticker on a Cadillac' was inspired by his driving one day down the San Diego Freeway and passing a Cadillac, the ultimate status symbol of right-wing upper-middle-class Americans. He was astonished to see it displaying a Deadhead sticker, something he regarded as his generation selling out. Although none of the other Eagles played on the 1984 original, they do an excellent job in recreating the instrumental subtleties of the song on this performance over 30 years later.

'Rocky Mountain Way' (Walsh/Roche Grace/Kenny Passarelli/Joe Vitale) 6.29

Written jointly by Walsh and the fellow members of Barnstorm, the band he formed on leaving The James Gang. In an interview on the *Howard Stern Show* in 2012, he described how the lyrics had come to him 40 years earlier. He said he was living in Colorado, mowing the lawn, looked up and saw the Front Range of the Rocky Mountains and was amazed to see that even in summer, they still had snow on them. The idea immediately came to him that the Rocky Mountain Way where he now lived was better than the way he had, because the music was better. 'Rocky Mountain Way is better than the way he had' immediately imprinted itself as on his mind as a chorus. Running indoors at once to write the words down, he forgot to shut off the lawnmower, which continued into his neighbour's yard and resulted in a large bill for the damage. Fortunately, the record was a hit, credited to Walsh alone and reaching number 23 in 1973. In Britain, it was released as a single in 1973 and 1975 without success, but during the short-lived craze for EPs in 1977, during the first year or so of 12" singles in Britain, it reappeared as one of four tracks on a 12" 45 and charted at number 39. One of the early air guitar favourites with that simple but effective riff, and also well ahead of its time in Walsh's use of voice box guitar, it was the closest to hard rock Eagles came in their stage show. As with 'Walk Away', their version was given added colour by the horn section.

Yet there would be more tours to come during the next few years, although the coronavirus pandemic of 2020–21 resulted in postponements of live music for artists across the world until after restrictions were lifted. The shows resumed in 2022, although there were indications that the end was drawing nigh for Eagles, as it was for many acts who had been in business since the late 1960s and early 1970s and had weathered many a change in personnel, with often only one original member fronting what the more critical punter might dismiss as almost a tribute band. (Step forward Status Quo, Steeleye Span and The Stranglers, for example.) Deacon Frey had announced in April that year how he was leaving for a solo career in order to 'forge his own path', but returned to join them as a special guest for a few numbers on their subsequent concerts that summer.

When they played at Anfield, Liverpool, on 20 June, Henley said to the audience that they were glad to be there – 'at this stage of the game, we're glad to be just about anywhere.' He promised them that there wouldn't be much talking, and no fireworks, no wind machines, no butt-waggling choreography, 'just a bunch of guys with guitars'. Towards the end of their performance at Hyde Park, London, six days later, he told them that just In case they didn't pass this way again, 'I want to thank you all for embracing these songs, taking them into your hearts and your homes – we appreciate it. It has been a hell of a ride!' It had indeed been a very long ride since they came to a cold wintry London some 50 years earlier to record that debut album.

Throughout that time, Eagles had scaled the peaks and plumbed the depths. They had gone from being the hottest ticket in town to the has-beens that nobody cared about – or would admit to caring about. Like ELO and ABBA, in the 21st century, in Britain, if not necessarily in America, they became one of the ultimate musical guilty secrets. In 2007 they received the ultimate backhanded compliment from Radiohead, who decided that just in case the master copy of their new album *In Rainbows* should fall into the wrong hands, they would write a name on the outside so nobody would bother to listen if they found it. The names they were sure would put any prospective listener off were *Eagles Greatest Hits*, *Kula Shaker Demos* and *Phil Collins Hip-Hop Covers*. As with that single line in *The Big Lebowski* some two decades earlier, any band who has reached the pinnacle sufficiently to become the butt of such jokes can surely take it as a compliment.

Songs performed live and early studio songs not officially released

A trawl of relevant sources online, including setlists and bootleg Tracklistings, gives some idea of songs that they played onstage but never recorded for release on vinyl or CD. These include cover versions of Chuck Berry's 'Oh Carol', a regular fixture in their setlist during the early years, Fats Domino's 'Walkin' to New Orleans', Neil Young's 'Ohio', Creedence Clearwater Revival's 'Have You Ever Seen the Rain', Huey 'Piano' Smith & his Clowns' 'Sea Cruise', 'Dream Baby', a hit on different occasions for Roy Orbison and Glen Campbell, and 'Deep in the Heart of Texas', recorded in the 1940s by several singers including Perry Como and Bing Crosby.

They also sometimes performed traditional numbers, including 'Silver Dagger' which was in their early days an a cappella intro for 'Take It Easy', 'Come All Ye Fair and Tender Ladies', 'Bonnie Galloway', and 'Blackberry Blossom'. A gig in Los Angeles in April 1974 has been bootlegged and also uploaded to YouTube. It includes Linda Ronstadt coming onstage to take lead vocal on 'Silver Threads and Golden Needles' (a song first recorded by Wanda Jackson in 1956, and later popularised in Britain by The Springfields) with the band, as well as 'It Doesn't Matter Anymore', the Paul Anka song made famous by Buddy Holly, with just her and Bernie Leadon accompanying themselves on acoustic guitars. She also joined them and Jackson Browne at the end on 'Take It Easy', again playing guitar. Discogs online lists several dozen 'unofficial' releases, with a cautionary note, that the site has blocked them from sale.

A list on Steve Hoffman Music Forums, dated 2011, names several songs – covers and originals – all apparently recorded at Wally Heider Sound Studios, San Francisco, probably early in 1972, and said to be possibly produced by Glyn Johns just before they made the first album with him at Olympic in Barnes, although the fact that he doesn't mention these sessions in his memoirs casts doubt on the theory. Among them are 'Oh Carol', Leadon's 'Rumble in the Tunnel', Souther's 'Caressa', 'You Drive Me Crazy' (which may be an alternative title for 'Get You in the Mood', the B-side of 'Take It Easy'), 'Fair and Tender Ladies', a slightly shortened title of the traditional song mentioned above, and 'You Don't Know Me', thought to be an early version of the much later Henley solo single 'You Don't Know Me At All'. 'Big River' and 'Lucifer' are assumed to be songs by Bob Seger from his 1970 album *Mongrel*, the latter number having received a new lease of life over 50 years later after appearing on Deep Purple's 2021 covers album, *Turning to Crime*. 'Night Owl', long predating the similarly named Gerry Rafferty hit, is probably another original, while 'Get Up, Kate' was a Frey song that he had performed with Linda Ronstadt's band. Barring one or two minor chords, it has a similar boogie shuffle tempo in the style of Loggins and Messina's 'Your Mama Don't Dance', later a hit for Poison.

Of particular interest are two more 'lost originals' from about a year later. They were both presumably meant to have been included on *On the Border*, which they were recording at the time, and they featured in the setlist of a show for a small crowd of about 1,500 at the College of the Holy Cross, Worcester, MA, in November 1973. One was 'Georgia Peach', written and sung by Leadon, a fast-paced rocker about three minutes long. The other was 'Wait and See' (or perhaps 'Oh Darlin', Wait and See'), a slower number written and sung by Meisner. About ten minutes long, it is a slow, ambitious piece sounding rather like Neil Young, with Meisner hitting the high notes a good deal, and several jamming passages. It appears that they never returned to either of these songs in the studio afterwards. The only recordings of them known to exist are poor-quality tapes presumably made by a member of the audience at the gig, both uploaded to the internet.

Resources

Books

Eliot, M., *To the Limit: The Untold Story of the Eagles* (Da Capo, 2005)

Felder, D., *Heaven and Hell: My Life in the Eagles (1974–2001)* (Weidenfeld & Nicolson, 2007)

Frame, P., *The Complete Rock Family Trees*, Vols. 1 & 2 (Omnibus, 1983)

Johns, G., *Sound Man* (Blue Rider, 2014)

Pidgeon, J., *Classic Albums: Interviews from the Radio 1 Series* (BBC, 1991)

Shapiro, M., *The Long Run: The Story of the Eagles* (Omnibus, 1995)

Thompson, D., *1000 Songs that Rock Your World* (Vintage, 2011)

Tobler, J. & Grundy, S., *The Record Producers* (BBC, 1982)

Vaughan, A., *The Eagles FAQ: All That's Left to Know about Classic Rock's Superstars* (Backbeat, 2015)

Articles and interviews

Bradley, L., 'An Eagle Lands' [interview with Glenn Frey] (*Independent*, 2 July 1992)

Brown, J., 'The Architect of 70's AOR: Bill Szymczyk on recording Joe Walsh, B.B. King, & the Eagles' (*Tape Op*, September/October 2014)

Browne, D., 'Eagles' Discography: Don Henley looks back' (*Rolling Stone*, 10 June 2016)

Browne, D. and others, 'The 40 Greatest Eagles Songs' (*Rolling Stone*, 22 September 2019)

Charlesworth, C., 'Where Eagles Dare' (*Melody Maker*, 11 December 1976)

Crowe, C., 'Chips off the old Buffalo' (*Rolling Stone*, 25 September 1975)

Everley, D., 'California Dreaming' (*Classic Rock*, December 2018)

Graff, G., 'The Eagles' 15 Best Songs: Critic's Picks' (*Billboard*, 17 October 2017)

Greene, A., 'Readers' Poll: The 10 Best Eagles Songs' (*Rolling Stone*, 29 July 2015)

Hasted, N., 'Take It Easy' (*Uncut*, February 2022)

Holloway, D., 'Eagles: Takin' it Easy' (*New Musical Express*, 10 March 1973)

Lester, P. 'Don Henley: "There's no partying, no alcohol, it's like a morgue backstage"' (*Guardian*, 1 October 2015)

Michaels, S., 'The Eagles' Don Henley accuses Frank Ocean and Okkervil River of song theft' (*Guardian*, 4 June 2014)

Plummer, M., 'Songs are so important' (*Melody Maker*, 3 March 1973)

Rensin, D., 'We were too busy trying to find a good restaurant' (*Crawdaddy*, July 1974)

Runtagh, J., 'The Eagles' "Hotel California": 10 Things You Didn't Know' (*Rolling Stone*, 6 December 2016)

Scoppa, B., 'Eagles' [review of first album] (*Rolling Stone*, 22 July 1972)

Various, 'The Ultimate Music Guide: Eagles' [including some articles cited above] (Uncut, May 2022)

Journals and newspapers
Classic Rock
Guardian
Melody Maker
Mojo
Musician
New Musical Express
Record Collector
Rolling Stone
Sounds
Uncut

Internet (accessed April–August 2022)
'Jessica', 'Wait & See': Randy's Lost Song & The College of the Holy Cross
(February 2022). Randy Meisner Retrospective
https://randymeisnerretrospective.com/2022/02/22/wait-see-randys-lost-song-
the-college-of-the-holy-cross/

Ozden, E.
The Reason Don Henley Mocked Robert Plant's Lack Of Vocal Capabilities
(October 2021). Rock Celebrities
https://rockcelebrities.net/the-reason-don-henley-mocked-robert-plants-lack-
of-vocal-capabilities/
-- Bernie Leadon Says The Eagles Became A 'Don Henley And Glenn Frey
Show' After The Second Album (January 2022), Rock Celebrities
https://rockcelebrities.net/bernie-leadon-says-the-eagles-became-a-don-felder-
and-glenn-frey-show-after-the-second-album

Rogovoy, S.
On Don Henley's birthday, the Secret Jewish History of the Eagles (July 2020).
Forward
https://forward.com/culture/451233/on-don-henleys-birthday-the-secret-
jewish-history-of-the-eagles/

Steve Hoffman Music Forums
https://forums.stevehoffman.tv/threads/unreleased-eagles-album.249438/

45cat.com vinyl database
allmusic.com
Discogs.com
Songfacts.com
vintagerock.com

The Eagles Albums – Best To Worst

Every Eagles fan has a different point of view, although the 'best album' is an almost unanimous choice – with mouth-watering sales figures to prove it. The 'worst' is by no means an unmitigated disaster, though the band admitted that creating it was an unhappy experience. After much humming, hawing, and exclusion for obvious reasons of the compilations, live and mostly live albums, the present author's choice is as follows:

1. Hotel California (1976)

1976, Henley said, was America's bicentennial year, and 'we figured since we are the Eagles and the Eagle is our national symbol, that we were obliged to make some kind of a little bicentennial statement using California as a microcosm of the whole United States.' The artistic pinnacle of their career opens with the adventurous, magnificently epic, lyrically challenging title track, and ends with the breathtaking 'Last Resort'. In between those benchmarks, it straddles country balladry in 'New Kid in Town', the yearning 'Philly soul torch song 'Wasted Time', and the searing guitar hero-meets-funk of' Life in the Fast Lane', while also showcasing the powerful guitar work of Felder in 'Victim of Love' and Walsh in 'Pretty Maids in a Row' respectively. It proved a hard, if not impossible, one to follow.

2. Desperado (1973)

Making your second album a more or less concept one, may sound pretentious on the face of it, but this wild west-themed set was soon acclaimed as something of a classic. The soothing 'Tequila Sunrise' and the much-covered poignant title track are the highlights of a record that rarely falls below standard, while the unashamedly loud 'Out of Control' shows they were a match for anybody in the air guitar stakes. Ironically, it was by some distance their lowest-charting studio album ever in the US.

3. One of These Nights (1975)

Their commercial breakthrough and first US chart-topping long player may have been the least 'rock' album they ever made, but with a title track that reached out into Al Green and Bee Gees territory and the prog-rock experiment that was the instrumental 'Journey of the Sorcerer', it demonstrates their capacity to break new ground, while keeping a foot in contemporary country rock with 'Lyin' Eyes', and delivering timeless balladry in Randy Meisner's finest moment, the sublime 'Take it to the Limit'.

4. Eagles (1972)

According to veteran music journalist Bud Scoppa, this debut was recorded when the band were operating as a democracy, and 'in their bright-eyed innocence [they made] the most balanced album they'd ever release, on their very first attempt.' Eoghan Lyng, in *Far Out*, ranks it their best as it 'showcase(s) a liveliness they would struggle to recapture on future albums .... virtually a live album in all but name', while Nick DeRiso, in *Classic Rock*, calls it their worst, 'bordering on blandness .... Too much country and not enough rock.' They were still finding their feet, but the freshness shines through on 'Take it Easy' and 'Peaceful Easy Feeling', while 'Witchy Woman' reveals a darker side that they would later exploit so well.

5. Long Road out of Eden (2007)

A latter-day equivalent of The Beatles' 'White Album', or Harrison's *All Things Must Pass*, their first studio double album and presumably their final studio one ever – a vast, sprawling soundscape that seems overwhelming on first listen. The weighty, Eastern-tinged 11-minute title track with Henley's acerbic commentary on the state of the world around him, the joyous if lyrically sombre 'How Long', a few tender love songs and some that reflect on concerns for their families, on ageing and (inevitably) on the environment, add up to a many-faceted collection that takes time to appreciate to the full.

6. On the Border (1974)

A transitional set, recorded while they were changing producers and recruiting another guitarist to lead them further into rock territory. The rather forced tribute 'James Dean' and a bold attempt at experimenting with R & B in the title track don't work too well, but there are triumphs in the exuberant 'Already Gone' and their first stateside number one, 'The Best of my Love', while Felder's guitar on 'Good Day in Hell' points towards a new direction.

7. The Long Run (1979)

By Henley's admission, the band had to follow up *Hotel California* at a time when they were 'physically, emotionally, spiritually and creatively exhausted'. 'Heartache Tonight' is by general critical consensus the highlight, and some of the other tracks are reasonable and at least passable, but the promising yet badly rushed 'Greeks Don't Want no Freaks', the woeful 'Teenage Jail' and the unpleasant 'Disco Strangler' all suggest that inspiration and quality control were lacking at least part of the time.

What Others Said About The Band

I still remember the first time I heard Don Henley and Glenn Frey, who became my backing band – I knew they were going to be massive stars. Can you believe it? I was so lucky to have Don and Glenn literally stood behind me on stage as I embarked on my career. Looking back, I probably knew that they would be the biggest American group of all time.
Linda Ronstadt

I knew [Glenn Frey] for 50 years. He was a great kid. I always kind of thought of him as my baby brother, a little bit. He was a joy to be around. I always looked forward to seeing him. It was always memorable. He had an amazing sense of humor and was just smart, whip-smart.
Bob Seger

It wasn't until I saw them in rehearsal, without a PA and without all the bad sound, that I realised their quality. The whole thing was that Glenn Frey wanted it to be a rock'n'roll band, and of course, that's what it became when I stopped producing them.
Glyn Johns

The Eagles and some others I would call bubblegum. [Their music has] got too much sugar in it. Life is tougher than they make it out to be.
Gram Parsons (Byrds, Flying Burrito Brothers)

When it comes to rock, pop music, whatever you want to call the genre, Don Henley is the finest vocalist there is. There's no question for me – he just has this amazing voice.
British DJ Johnnie Walker

You can't deny that these guys have written the American songbook.
Paul Stanley (Kiss)

The Eagles helped shape my understanding of music when I was growing up.
Dave Navarro (Jane's Addiction, Red Hot Chili Peppers)

Eagles released my favourite album of all time, *Hotel California*.
Meat Loaf

My mom used to play Eagles records for me on my way to grade school. We lost one of the greatest songwriters ever today.
Justin Timberlake (in a tribute to Glenn Frey)

On Track series

Allman Brothers Band – Andrew Wild 978-1-78952-252-5
Tori Amos – Lisa Torem 978-1-78952-142-9
Asia – Peter Braidis 978-1-78952-099-6
Badfinger – Robert Day-Webb 978-1-878952-176-4
Barclay James Harvest – Keith and Monica Domone 978-1-78952-067-5
The Beatles – Andrew Wild 978-1-78952-009-5
The Beatles Solo 1969-1980 – Andrew Wild 978-1-78952-030-9
Blue Oyster Cult – Jacob Holm-Lupo 978-1-78952-007-1
Blur – Matt Bishop 978-178952-164-1
Marc Bolan and T.Rex – Peter Gallagher 978-1-78952-124-5
Kate Bush – Bill Thomas 978-1-78952-097-2
Camel – Hamish Kuzminski 978-1-78952-040-8
Captain Beefheart – Opher Goodwin 978-1-78952-235-8
Caravan – Andy Boot 978-1-78952-127-6
Cardiacs – Eric Benac 978-1-78952-131-3
Nick Cave and The Bad Seeds – Dominic Sanderson 978-1-78952-240-2
Eric Clapton Solo – Andrew Wild 978-1-78952-141-2
The Clash – Nick Assirati 978-1-78952-077-4
Crosby, Stills and Nash – Andrew Wild 978-1-78952-039-2
Creedence Clearwater Revival – Tony Thompson 978-178952-237-2
The Damned – Morgan Brown 978-1-78952-136-8
Deep Purple and Rainbow 1968-79 – Steve Pilkington 978-1-78952-002-6
Dire Straits – Andrew Wild 978-1-78952-044-6
The Doors – Tony Thompson 978-1-78952-137-5
Dream Theater – Jordan Blum 978-1-78952-050-7
Eagles – John Van der Kiste 978-1-78952-260-0
Electric Light Orchestra – Barry Delve 978-1-78952-152-8
Elvis Costello and The Attractions – Georg Purvis 978-1-78952-129-0
Emerson Lake and Palmer – Mike Goode 978-1-78952-000-2
Fairport Convention – Kevan Furbank 978-1-78952-051-4
Peter Gabriel – Graeme Scarfe 978-1-78952-138-2
Genesis – Stuart MacFarlane 978-1-78952-005-7
Gentle Giant – Gary Steel 978-1-78952-058-3
Gong – Kevan Furbank 978-1-78952-082-8
Hall and Oates – Ian Abrahams 978-1-78952-167-2
Hawkwind – Duncan Harris 978-1-78952-052-1
Peter Hammill – Richard Rees Jones 978-1-78952-163-4
Roy Harper – Opher Goodwin 978-1-78952-130-6
Jimi Hendrix – Emma Stott 978-1-78952-175-7
The Hollies – Andrew Darlington 978-1-78952-159-7
The Human League and The Sheffield Scene – Andrew Darlington 978-1-78952-186-3
Iron Maiden – Steve Pilkington 978-1-78952-061-3
Jefferson Airplane – Richard Butterworth 978-1-78952-143-6
Jethro Tull – Jordan Blum 978-1-78952-016-3
Elton John in the 1970s – Peter Kearns 978-1-78952-034-7
The Incredible String Band – Tim Moon 978-1-78952-107-8
Iron Maiden – Steve Pilkington 978-1-78952-061-3
Joe Jackson – Richard James 978-1-78952-189-4
Billy Joel – Lisa Torem 978-1-78952-183-2
Judas Priest – John Tucker 978-1-78952-018-7
Kansas – Kevin Cummings 978-1-78952-057-6
The Kinks – Martin Hutchinson 978-1-78952-172-6
Korn – Matt Karpe 978-1-78952-153-5
Led Zeppelin – Steve Pilkington 978-1-78952-151-1

Level 42 – Matt Philips 978-1-78952-102-3
Little Feat – Georg Purvis - 978-1-78952-168-9
Aimee Mann – Jez Rowden 978-1-78952-036-1
Joni Mitchell – Peter Kearns 978-1-78952-081-1
The Moody Blues – Geoffrey Feakes 978-1-78952-042-2
Motorhead – Duncan Harris 978-1-78952-173-3
Nektar – Scott Meze – 978-1-78952-257-0
New Order – Dennis Remmer – 979-1-78952-249-5
Laura Nyro – Philip Ward 978-1-78952-182-5
Mike Oldfield – Ryan Yard 978-1-78952-060-6
Opeth – Jordan Blum 978-1-78-952-166-5
Pearl Jam – Ben L. Connor 978-1-78952-188-7
Tom Petty – Richard James 978-1-78952-128-3
Pink Floyd – 978-1-78952-242-6 Richard Butterworth
Porcupine Tree – Nick Holmes 978-1-78952-144-3
Queen – Andrew Wild 978-1-78952-003-3
Radiohead – William Allen 978-1-78952-149-8
Rancid – Paul Matts 989-1-78952-187-0
Renaissance – David Detmer 978-1-78952-062-0
The Rolling Stones 1963-80 – Steve Pilkington 978-1-78952-017-0
The Smiths and Morrissey – Tommy Gunnarsson 978-1-78952-140-5
Spirit – Rev. Keith A. Gordon – 978-1-78952- 248-8
Stackridge – Alan Draper 978-1-78952-232-7
Status Quo the Frantic Four Years – Richard James 978-1-78952-160-3
Steely Dan – Jez Rowden 978-1-78952-043-9
Steve Hackett – Geoffrey Feakes 978-1-78952-098-9
Tears For Fears – Paul Clark - 978-178952-238-9
Thin Lizzy – Graeme Stroud 978-1-78952-064-4
Tool – Matt Karpe 978-1-78952-234-1
Toto – Jacob Holm-Lupo 978-1-78952-019-4
U2 – Eoghan Lyng 978-1-78952-078-1
UFO – Richard James 978-1-78952-073-6
Van Der Graaf Generator – Dan Coffey 978-1-78952-031-6
Van Halen – Morgan Brown – 9781-78952-256-3
The Who – Geoffrey Feakes 978-1-78952-076-7
Roy Wood and the Move – James R Turner 978-1-78952-008-8
Yes – Stephen Lambe 978-1-78952-001-9
Frank Zappa 1966 to 1979 – Eric Benac 978-1-78952-033-0
Warren Zevon – Peter Gallagher 978-1-78952-170-2
10CC – Peter Kearns 978-1-78952-054-5

Decades Series
The Bee Gees in the 1960s – Andrew Mon Hughes et al 978-1-78952-148-1
The Bee Gees in the 1970s – Andrew Mon Hughes et al 978-1-78952-179-5
Black Sabbath in the 1970s – Chris Sutton 978-1-78952-171-9
Britpop – Peter Richard Adams and Matt Pooler 978-1-78952-169-6
Phil Collins in the 1980s – Andrew Wild 978-1-78952-185-6
Alice Cooper in the 1970s – Chris Sutton 978-1-78952-104-7
Curved Air in the 1970s – Laura Shenton 978-1-78952-069-9
Donovan in the 1960s – Jeff Fitzgerald 978-1-78952-233-4
Bob Dylan in the 1980s – Don Klees 978-1-78952-157-3
Brian Eno in the 1970s – Gary Parsons 978-1-78952-239-6
Faith No More in the 1990s – Matt Karpe 978-1-78952-250-1
Fleetwood Mac in the 1970s – Andrew Wild 978-1-78952-105-4
Fleetwood Mac in the 1980s – Don Klees 978-178952-254-9

Focus in the 1970s – Stephen Lambe 978-1-78952-079-8
Free and Bad Company in the 1970s – John Van der Kiste 978-1-78952-178-8
Genesis in the 1970s – Bill Thomas 978178952-146-7
George Harrison in the 1970s – Eoghan Lyng 978-1-78952-174-0
Kiss in the 1970s – Peter Gallagher 978-1-78952-246-4
Manfred Mann's Earth Band in the 1970s – John Van der Kiste 978178952-243-3
Marillion in the 1980s – Nathaniel Webb 978-1-78952-065-1
Van Morrison in the 1970s – Peter Childs - 978-1-78952-241-9
Mott the Hoople and Ian Hunter in the 1970s – John Van der Kiste 978-1-78-952-162-7
Pink Floyd In The 1970s – Georg Purvis 978-1-78952-072-9
Suzi Quatro in the 1970s – Darren Johnson 978-1-78952-236-5
Roxy Music in the 1970s – Dave Thompson 978-1-78952-180-1
Status Quo in the 1980s – Greg Harper 978-1-78952-244-0
Tangerine Dream in the 1970s – Stephen Palmer 978-1-78952-161-0
The Sweet in the 1970s – Darren Johnson 978-1-78952-139-9
Uriah Heep in the 1970s – Steve Pilkington 978-1-78952-103-0
Van der Graaf Generator in the 1970s – Steve Pilkington 978-1-78952-245-7
Yes in the 1980s – Stephen Lambe with David Watkinson 978-1-78952-125-2

On Screen series
Carry On… – Stephen Lambe 978-1-78952-004-0
David Cronenberg – Patrick Chapman 978-1-78952-071-2
Doctor Who: The David Tennant Years – Jamie Hailstone 978-1-78952-066-8
James Bond – Andrew Wild 978-1-78952-010-1
Monty Python – Steve Pilkington 978-1-78952-047-7
Seinfeld Seasons 1 to 5 – Stephen Lambe 978-1-78952-012-5

Other Books
1967: A Year In Psychedelic Rock 978-1-78952-155-9
1970: A Year In Rock – John Van der Kiste 978-1-78952-147-4
1973: The Golden Year of Progressive Rock 978-1-78952-165-8
Babysitting A Band On The Rocks – G.D. Praetorius 978-1-78952-106-1
Eric Clapton Sessions – Andrew Wild 978-1-78952-177-1
Derek Taylor: For Your Radioactive Children – Andrew Darlington 978-1-78952-038-5
The Golden Road: The Recording History of The Grateful Dead – John Kilbride 978-1-78952-156-6
Iggy and The Stooges On Stage 1967-1974 – Per Nilsen 978-1-78952-101-6
Jon Anderson and the Warriors – the road to Yes – David Watkinson 978-1-78952-059-0
Misty: The Music of Johnny Mathis – Jakob Baekgaard 978-1-78952-247-1
Nu Metal: A Definitive Guide – Matt Karpe 978-1-78952-063-7
Tommy Bolin: In and Out of Deep Purple – Laura Shenton 978-1-78952-070-5
Maximum Darkness – Deke Leonard 978-1-78952-048-4
The Twang Dynasty – Deke Leonard 978-1-78952-049-1

and many more to come!

Would you like to write for Sonicbond Publishing?

At Sonicbond Publishing we are always on the look-out for authors, particularly for our two main series:

On Track. Mixing fact with in depth analysis, the On Track series examines the work of a particular musical artist or group. All genres are considered from easy listening and jazz to 60s soul to 90s pop, via rock and metal.

On Screen. This series looks at the world of film and television. Subjects considered include directors, actors and writers, as well as entire television and film series. As with the On Track series, we balance fact with analysis.

While professional writing experience would, of course, be an advantage the most important qualification is to have real enthusiasm and knowledge of your subject. First-time authors are welcomed, but the ability to write well in English is essential.

Sonicbond Publishing has distribution throughout Europe and North America, and all books are also published in E-book form. Authors will be paid a royalty based on sales of their book.

Further details are available from www.sonicbondpublishing.co.uk. To contact us, complete the contact form there or email info@sonicbondpublishing.co.uk

Follow us on social media:
Twitter: https://twitter.com/SonicbondP
Instagram: https://www.instagram.com/sonicbondpublishing_/
Facebook: https://www.facebook.com/SonicbondPublishing/

Linktree QR code: